John Thomas Trimble

BROADMAN PRESS
Nashville, Tennessee

© Copyright 1978 • Broadman Press
All rights reserved.
4256–24
ISBN: 0–8054–5624–4

Dewey Decimal Classification: 301.42
Subject heading: MARRIAGE
Library of Congress Catalog Card Number: 77–073452
Printed in the United States of America.

*To my wife, I'Lee
with whom I have shared
marriage intimacy*

Acknowledgments

I wish to express my deep appreciation to several who have directly or indirectly contributed to the completion of this work. First I want to acknowledge the vision of The Board of Managers of The Missouri Baptist Children's Home, where I now minister. They see my mission as being broad rather than as narrow and limited. Because of this perception, I am supported by them in the writing of this book. This permits me to use more fully the gifts with which I feel most comfortable.

I also want to express my appreciation, admiration, and respect for my dear friend, Howard L. Meyer, administrator of The Missouri Baptist Children's Home. It is because of his active encouragement and genuine support that I am given the opportunity to make this kind of contribution. It is indeed good to work for and with a friend in a community of friends. Such relationships I have found at The Missouri Baptist Children's Home.

Several others have contributed more directly to the completion of this book. For them I am grateful. Those typists who have helped include: Debbie Wiens, Debbie Williams, Sandy Volner, Gerri Ball, Lindy Land, and Cherry Davidson. Elaine Auch assisted in the coordination of the typing and other assignments.

Finally, to my family I say one more "thank you" for understanding the importance of writing to me. Of course, they have lived with me long enough to know that this is part of my life, and so we try to intensify our relationship in other ways at other times. Acceptance of my work by them is precious to me. And so to I'Lee, Sherry, John, and Vince—thank you.

Introduction

Writing about intimacy is like trying to capture a cloud. As with clouds no one questions the existence of intimacy, but both are most difficult to capture.

So I have attempted to arrive at the meaning of intimacy in very much the same way as I might attempt to capture a cloud. My strategy has been to attempt to surround the meaning of intimacy and then to close in on it, trying to be careful not to lose any important parts. Intimacy represents for us what we consider to be a peak human experience; thus, as with any ideal, we can only hope to come close to its meaning.

My mission might be summarized best as an attempt to provide *perspective* on the experience of intimacy.

I feel I have been true to the truth (99 percent of the time!). I've tried to write what I felt the truth of an issue might be, even though my conclusion might not be what some would prefer to hear. I want to be sure that, if my efforts have succeeded to encourage some to reach for intimacy who otherwise would not have ventured forth, I have made them fully aware of the dimensions of the task which lies before them also. I want them to be as fully equipped for their journey as possible.

I hope that what I have written will encourage others to *inspire themselves* to work on and to achieve intimacy. *I* certainly have no power to inspire another person, nor can anyone else do so. I may be able to stimulate a response in them which helps them to inspire themselves, but the power belongs to them alone. I respect that boundary.

I have entitled the book *Intimacy in Marriage* for specific reasons. First let me clarify what I do *not* mean to imply by the title. I am not assuming that marriage is the *only* place intimacy can or should occur. But I do believe that marriage is the institution in which most intimacy is experienced. I believe that marriage is the best place for intimacy to grow, to be maintained, and to be revived should it fall victim to neglect.

Marriage, whatever else it may be, is the formalized relationship between two people who have made a great personal commitment to each other. Something as important as marriage should be entered into only after one has achieved a *full* awareness of its deepest meaning. Yet, we all know that often marriage is not born in that manner. This accounts for many of the problems which exist in marriage today.

I find it difficult to believe that an alternate life-style to marriage is the answer for the problems which exist in marriage. Rather, I believe the answer lies in a clearer understanding of the meaning and significance of the marriage relationship. Alternate life-styles to marriage often are espoused by those who have trapped themselves into a relationship they realize they never should have chosen in the first place. Many who would not be able to adjust themselves to the marriage relationship with *any* person also see good things in an alternative to marriage. Some who do realize the serious meaning of marriage, but who fear that they would not be adequate for such an important human relationship, also see much value in an alternative to marriage. They are often threat-sensitive and dominated by feelings of inadequacy. And of course there are also healthy experimenters who simply want to find out for themselves the range of choices they have available to them in relationships. Most will eventually choose marriage. By entitling the book *Intimacy in Marriage,* I want to emphasize my strong belief in the value of the marriage relationship. I believe it is the *best* place for intimacy to grow for *most* people.

However, I do not confine my discussion of intimacy to the intimacy which occurs only within marriage. Intimacy is a *human* relational event. Marriage is an institutionalization of a human relationship. But I'm concerned with intimacy wherever it may occur. Some have divorced and yet seek intimacy. Others will divorce because of a lack of felt intimacy and will begin to look for intimacy. Many have not yet married and look for intimacy. Some will never marry—perhaps by choice, perhaps not—but they too seek intimacy. My book is for *everyone* who seeks intimacy.

At the end of each chapter there are a few questions for discussion and some exercises for individuals, couples, or groups to do in order to go more deeply into the issues raised in that chapter.

In one sense, this is a book on conservation—conservation of a word which depicts a very beautiful and special experience—one we call intimacy. In metaphor, I'm attempting to save the word for future generations from the carelessness of man who would call almost any experience of closeness by its name. I would save the purity of the species of the word from inbreeding with partially similar, but intrinsically different, experiences.

I wish to avoid for the experience of intimacy what has happened to its now nearly extinct sister—*love*. The experience of love now has so many names that only the foolish would rush in to attempt an exposition on the definition of its essential meaning. The word *love* has been reduced primarily to an expression of a personal feeling, and it is used almost promiscuously. I do not want this to happen to *intimacy*. I want to conserve its special meaning.

I have taken a descriptive approach in contrast to what I might call a prescriptive or moralistic stance. In the descriptive approach we do not deal with shoulds and oughts. Rather, the emphasis is on the description of human behavior.

It is not that there are no shoulds and oughts—a Christian cannot believe that! I do believe in personal accountability for our behavior—to God primarily. But I do not wish to deal with such issues in this book, as important as they may be. And so I've limited my discussions here to my perception of how people behave with respect to intimacy. I shall leave the evaluation of whether that behavior is right or wrong to someone else who feels more qualified to do that than I.

I am appreciative of the efforts of others who have written in this field. I respect their wisdom and admire their courage to write about intimacy. In my review of the literature, I have become aware that perhaps the greatest contributions have been made by a handful of people. It is said that new achievements are not produced solely by individuals but rather that we stand on the shoulders of giants. I would like to pause for a moment and salute a few giants.

This list could be long, of course, unless I were selective and chose a few from among the many. Obviously the selection is personal, based on my private perception. I salute first of all Charlotte and Howard Clinebell whose book *The Intimate Marriage* stands as a landmark pointing in the direction of the truth about intimacy and marriage. I also salute Thomas C. Oden who pursued in depth the meaning of intimacy in his book *Game Free*. Paul Tournier has contributed much to Christian literature from the standpoint of those of us in the behavioral sciences. I praise him for two of his books, *To Understand Each Other* and *Secrets*. I also thank Jerry Greenwald for the insights he has contributed in his offering, *Creative Intimacy*.

I've stood on such shoulders as I wrote this book. I can only hope that my contribution will be such that I too shall be able to assist another to stand upon my shoulders—to whatever height that may extend him—to see the truth in God more clearly.

Contents

1. The Nature and Meaning of Intimacy   *15*
2. The Intimacy Workshop   *28*
3. The Ingredients of Intimacy   *52*
4. Exercises in Intimacy   *73*
5. How Often Is Intimacy Achieved?   *109*

1. The Nature and Meaning of Intimacy

The Case of Bill and Mary

They were at a party. Each one knew a few of the others who had come to celebrate the announcement which was to be made later that evening—but everyone knew what was to be said. Then they met. Whether it was totally a chance meeting or whether it was some perception at deeper levels of consciousness which brought them together was unknown and unimportant. As they greeted each other politely and properly, something else was happening and they both knew it. It was easy to maintain eye contact for long periods of time, and a smile seemed to be the only appropriate reaction. Talk was small and casual, but easy—although with some delightfully pleasant nervousness.

They talked to each other for the rest of the evening, seeming to move rather rapidly to the sharing of more and more personal information about themselves. They were surprised at how quickly the moments passed. As the time arrived when it would be embarrassing for them not to say good-bye, they shook hands—more for the opportunity to touch each other than for the social amenity, looked deeply into each other's eyes with the penetrating message of the full awareness of the presence of the other, and then slowly and reluctantly said their farewells. The final contact of their hands was broken; their eyes finished the wordless parting; and they turned and walked away.

Can two people who are strangers, two people who do not know each other well, experience deep feelings of closeness for each other? Even though the reasons for such an uncommon and deep attraction are far beyond their awarenesses, can these feelings legitimately be called *intimate?* Many would call this kind of experience intimate; others would not.

The word *intimate* has been used often and applied widely with little precision in its definition. If we are to invest a significant amount of energy in the pursuit of the meaning of intimacy, it is essential to define as clearly as we can what kind of experience we are speaking of when we use the word.

My attempts to define words in this book and to try to distinguish one word from another are directed toward the *experience* behind the words we use. We cannot understand our experiences if we do not label them well and thereby attempt to differentiate one experience from another. So, if we can label an experience in such a way as to differentiate it from all other experiences, I think we can evaluate our experiences more effectively, and this will help us more fully take control of our lives.

Although *intimacy* is difficult to define—as witness the few attempts to do so—I feel the effort must be made. The social linguist theorist in the behavioral sciences holds that if a person cannot explain an idea, he does not really know it. Whether that is true or not, I do believe it would be worth the time and effort to struggle to define intimacy for the purpose of clarity of communication.

I would not presume to suppose that everyone will agree with the definition at which I will arrive, but at least everyone will know fairly clearly the experience to which I allude in my further discussions of intimacy. So, where shall we begin? I would propose that we begin with what is perhaps the most objective definition of intimacy we can find and move on from there.

Building Some Fences to Surround the Meaning

The dictionary tells us what our society generally has agreed to let the word *intimacy* mean in its most basic sense. We cannot rightfully change the accepted meaning of a word in the English vocabulary simply because it fits our need, else we will become lost in a Babel of confusion. There *are* certain agreed-to meanings of a word as used by people, and we *must* pay respectful attention to that. So let us begin with this rather objective frame of reference and then proceed to expand or modify the meaning from that; yet we should not stray too far from these commonly accepted language anchors. Another thing—the definition we arrive at must tell both what intimacy *is* and what it *is not,* so we will be able to evaluate an experience by a careful comparison of that experience with each of the elements in its definition.

The Problem with Dictionaries

Several dictionaries [1,2] indicate that the word intimate is derived from the Latin word *intimatus* which literally means "put or pressed into" in the sense of being pressed into the inmost part. Applying this to persons, we can infer that it has the sense of being part of the inmost or most essential part of a person. It is intrinsic to the nature of that person. It lies deep within the individual and is most private. The dictionaries also indicate that the word involves a warm and personally close association that is long-standing. It also includes the knowledge which arises from that close association in human experience. Finally, one dictionary [3] adds another meaning which seems at first to be out of character with what has preceded up to this point. It indicates that the word is also used to refer to *illicit* sexual relations.

All meanings of *intimate* seem quite harmonious and positive until we reach this aspect of the definition. The most puzzling thing at first glance would seem to be not the inclusion of sex as a part of the meaning of intimacy but the fact that it is characterized as *illicit*.

I think the dictionary is quite correct to include this idea of illicit sex as part of the accepted definition of intimacy, for I believe it is in keeping with the way people use the word.

When a teary-eyed wife asks a husband, whose attentions have wandered from her to another woman, if he has been "intimate" with the other woman, she is not asking if he has *knowledge* of the inmost, intrinsic nature of the personality of the woman! She is not asking primarily if he has had a long and warm nonsexual association with her—although that may be another question she may soon be asking. No, in most cases she is really asking whether he has had sex with her.

Most persons would agree that in *this* particular context of the meaning of intimate, the reference is to culturally defined *illicit* sex—and that's why it is included in the definition. We must keep in mind the fact that the dictionary does not give us the kind of definition we will need for this study. It does not tell us, logically and tightly, what is and what is not intimacy. Rather, it merely reports all the ways people use the word. The dictionary reflects whatever confusion exists in the minds of people as they use the word. We can use the dictionary as a starting point but we must go on from there to complete the picture.

We first need to identify the *experiences* behind the various usages of the word and then look for the central core of meaning which binds them all together. And so we observe that many people in their minds tie sex to intimacy. Sometimes it is seen as beautiful, and sometimes it is viewed as illicit.

But why is this so? What must be in the minds of people for them to have this double impression? Here I can only resort to the use of my clinical judgment in order to evaluate what *might* be going on. First, my guess is that the way people tie sex and intimacy together involves in some way a distinction they could be making between marital and nonmarital sex. My hypothesis runs something like this.

Society (that great impersonal composite of social opinion and pressure to conform) views marital sex as the relationship which is most compatible with intimacy, for in marriage one has every opportunity to know the other person deeply over a long period of time. If this is true, then society would also view nonmarital sex as incompatible with intimacy for these reasons. First, if we are speaking of extramarital sex, then this kind of a relationship would be seen as competing with marital intimacy and is thus illicit from society's point of view. Second, if on the other hand we are speaking of nonmarital sex, then this also might be seen to be incompatible with intimacy not only because it often implies an exploitation of one person by another but also because it often is a very temporary relationship. Nonmarital sex may not, and often does not, lead to marriage. Thus, sex outside of marriage is viewed by many in our society as illicit, and this is why it is included in a dictionary definition of intimacy.

Do the Facts Fit the Fantasy of Society?

To what do the observed facts testify? Many contradictions! First of all, sex in many marriages today is anything but intimate. Second, many unmarried persons testify that they do experience intimacy when they have sex with someone special with whom they have had a relationship for a period of time. At least that's what they *do* say. Third, for every exploiter there is an exploitee waiting around to have his loser's script fulfilled. It takes two to accomplish an exploitation, and some degree of cooperation at some level of consciousness. Fourth, every permanent relationship has to begin sometime with a temporary relationship, and so a temporary relationship may become a permanent relationship—a marital relationship. The conclusion? Confusion!

In my opinion, sex has become the (imperfect and improper)

symbol of intimacy to many people. So when the woman, in my previous illustration, asks the man if he has been intimate with the other woman, she probably means primarily *sexual* relations, but she may also have in mind that he might have entered into several other spheres of intimacy with the other person—areas of life which she had previously considered especially hers alone.

If an individual has sex with another person, he has entered a very private area of that person's life; consequently, great closeness *can* occur. However, the fact is that sexual relations do not always bring two people closer. Sometimes the opposite it true.

Sex and intimacy are only moderately related. Sex is a sharpening factor. There is nothing intrinsically intimate about sex, although there is much that is private and personal. But sex *does amplify* an already existing relationship; it can make it better or much worse.

Similar Words and Experiences

There are a few kindred words which need to be nailed down with fairly precise descriptions so we will not dilute our definition of intimacy. I believe it would make sense to use the words *erotic* and *sensual* to describe those times when we experience sexual feelings without a sense of personal closeness. For those times when we feel very close to another person without an accompanying sexual relationship and without a developed relationship, we might label the experience as *soul-touching*. I shall reserve the word *ecstasy* for those times when one experiences soul-touching and also expresses it through sexual relations but without there being a developed relationship.

Those who have written about intimacy have offered descriptions which are very similar in many respects. They stress closeness, sharing, a developed relationship, growing, and other dimensions they believe to be important aspects of intimacy.

However, none of the writers have attempted to define intimacy in any kind of categorical sense—in a way whereby it could be used as a kind of measuring stick for the identification and evaluation of a potentially intimate experience and of a possible intimate relationship. I shall attempt to provide that possibly missing element.

I shall present a definition that can be used as a fairly objective frame of reference in order to communicate more clearly what we mean when we refer to the experience of intimacy. It will help us evaluate what we observe, what we experience, and what we read about intimacy.

I realize that such an approach is not what might be called an inspirational one. I am well aware that some would much rather let the contemplation of intimacy inspire them and make them feel good. I think there is a legitimate place for such meditation. But I see my task as returning to the foundations of meaning so when we are indeed inspired, it will have been by something we can touch and nourish. I do stress the feeling aspect of intimacy, of course, and I too am awed by the beauty of the experience itself. I am sure that at least some of this will show. It is my hope that after the clarification process, all of us will have a new space in which to experience and evaluate intimacy in our lives.

A Categorical Definition of Intimacy

I propose for my definition of intimacy the following: *Intimacy is a vivid feeling of closeness arising from a purposefully selected and developed, mutually committed, adult relationship.* In this definition I mean to emphasize seven major elements: (a) the feeling aspect; (b) the experience of closeness; (c) the development of the relationship; (d) purposeful selection; (e) mutuality of feeling; (f) mutuality of commitment; (g) an adult experience.

Let's examine each aspect in some detail to see why I consider each to be essential elements of the definition.

Feeling

The first element is *feeling*. The feeling emphasis makes intimacy a private and personally judged experience. The individual remains king of his own consciousness. No intruders are allowed to determine for him the meaning of his own experience, for it is rightfully his and his alone. I affirm the right of the individual to have the last word about his own experience. If all other elements of the definition are "in place" and yet the individual feels nothing, he casts the deciding vote against that experience being an intimate one.

Closeness

The second element is the experience of *closeness*. This part of the definition focuses upon that almost indescribable, and certainly undefinable, aspect of intimacy to which many writers have devoted so much time.

"It is the true season of love when we know that we alone can love, that no one could ever have loved before us and that no one will ever love in the same way after us."—Johann Wolfgang Von Goethe

"There is a sense among intimates that they share something that is unique to them and them alone." [4]

And two lines from Mignon McLaughlin's *The Neurotic's Notebook*—"Love is the silent saying and saying again of a single name" [5] and "She loves him if, even when she's not thinking about him, she's thinking about him." [6]

I could add to these the much more prolonged descriptions that other writers have provided.

A Developed Relationship

The third aspect of my definition is that there must be some kind of *developed relationship* out of which the feeling of closeness arises. When we examine the intimate relationship, it must be evaluated on the basis both of quantity and quality. Without an adequate opportunity for the development of the relationship, intimacy has little chance to live. Without more than a few efforts at producing feelings of closeness the probabilities are lowered significantly for the development of intimacy.

On the other hand, just to log time with another person is obviously inadequate. To achieve a hundred neutral experiences is like adding zeros and hoping to arrive at more than zero. Intimacy does not derive merely from accumulated experience, but rather from a *special* kind of experience—one characterized by feelings of closeness. What occurs *during* the time together is of utmost importance. That is why I have used the qualifying word *developed* when I refer to an intimate relationship, signifying both a significant amount of time and growth during that time. How much time is definitely related to what happens during that period.

If the idea of a developed relationship were not included in the definition, it would leave room for the definition of intimacy to include those undeniable experiences of felt closeness with a previously unknown person. These may occur either because two thirsty and deprived souls meet at a timely moment for both or because certain aspects of each other remind each of someone else with whom they had previously experienced intimacy. This kind of relationship is based more upon fantasy than upon reality. If the dimension of a developed relationship is included in the definition of intimacy, then until the relationship develops further—as a result of purposeful interactions in depth—the immediate feeling of closeness to a stranger would qualify only as "soul-touching" or perhaps "ecstacy," if sex were added to the encounter. It will be remembered that this is how I described these two terms earlier.

Purposeful Selection

The fourth part of my definition is that intimacy is an experience that is *purposefully selected.* Here I am emphasizing the fact that out of the many experiences we have with other persons, we tend to focus our attention and energy upon one particular person. The choosing is an active process, not a reactive one. The selection activates the needs and desires throughout the various levels of consciousness of a person—his unconscious, his subconscious, and his consciousness awareness—as we respond for reasons we cannot tell but which are powerfully persuasive and undeniable. The choice proceeds from the innermost part of ourselves to the other person rather than from a defensive, coping reaction to some outside event or situation.

One thing I am attempting to do with this element of the definition is to rule out any feelings of closeness two persons might experience with each other as a result of each having suffered at some time, recent or remote, some common, unpredictable external crisis event in their lives—a death, an accident, a divorce, an illness. I feel that this *reactive*, clinging response does not characterize intimacy, although it may indeed result in a close, deeply felt fellowship of suffering. Such events certainly have, many times before, brought together perfect strangers—sometimes literally "strange bedfellows" in their suffering; but it does not, in my opinion, qualify as intimacy. Another good example is "love on the rebound." Here the response is clinging in nature and reactive to the pain of a deeply felt loss. Intimacy must be purposefully and voluntarily chosen.

Mutuality of Feeling

The fifth element of the definition is *mutuality of feeling*. Is it possible for one person to experience intimacy while the other person does not? I don't think so. I think intimacy has to be a two-way experience. However, I do not think a given experience within an intimate relationship has to be fully mutual for intimacy to be experienced. Let me elaborate.

While two people need not experience the *same level* of feelings of closeness *at the same time,* they must both be *open* to these feelings; they must at least occasionally experience deep feelings of closeness for each other. There can be individual differences here. For example, one individual may *feel* the closeness of the relationship much more intensely than the other person most of the time. Or the two may alternate in their feelings so that for a time he might experience more feelings of closeness than she does, and then for another period of time she experiences them more. The important thing is that no matter what the pattern, both have the experience. An intimate experience cannot be a one-way event, for in knowing the innermost part of another, there must be a reciprocal openness to let another person in.

Mutual Commitment

The sixth element of the definition is *mutual commitment.* The couple must make some kind of specific and felt commitment of themselves to each other. Commitment implies that the relationship will last long enough for intimacy to have the opportunity to grow and to develop. Different people make different levels of commitment to each other. Generally speaking, the greater the commitment in terms of time, energy, and intensity, the greater is the opportunity for the development of intimacy, and often the more deeply the intimate experience will be felt. A limited commitment will produce a limited experience, assuming that there is at least enough experience (however much that may be) to result in at least minimal levels of intimacy.

An Adult Experience

The final element in the definition is that the experience must be *an adult experience.* It requires growth and maturity to be able to get in touch with the innermost part of another person and to know one's self sufficiently to be able to experience intimacy.

This then is my definition of intimacy, written after a careful review of the excellent thinking of other authors, and after a personally painstaking effort to try to arrive at the basic essentials. One might argue endlessly as to what is the "correct" or "best" definition of intimacy. I have, of course, presented what I believe to be correct; however, to be able to prove its validity is not as important to me as the fact that I have tried to make my frame of reference as explicit as possible so I may be understood better in the other things I have to say about intimacy in this work. My further comments derive from the basic frame of reference laid down in this first chapter.

What Do You Think?

1. My purpose in defining intimacy as I did was to separate out, as best I could, the *experience* of intimacy from all other human experiences. Using my definition, can you think of any other human experience which also would be described by my definition of intimacy? If so, what are those experiences and what needs to be added to or subtracted from my definition in order to make the experience of intimacy unique? Is intimacy a unique experience in your opinion, or is it merely a synonym for some other experience?

2. Do you think it is appropriate to include in the definition of intimacy the element of a *developed* relationship? Could it be eliminated and a meaningful definition of intimacy remain intact? What are the consequences or implications for the meaning of intimacy if the element of a developed relationship is *not* included as part of the definition?

3. Ask five people you know to define intimacy in any way they want to and see if you find some confusion about the meaning of intimacy. Perhaps, on the other hand, you will find some fair agreement as to its meaning. As you do your survey, be sure to ask them specifically to tell you what role they feel sex plays in intimacy. Compare the *elements* of their descriptions to the elements in my definition and see what is missing, if anything. Arrive at your own conclusion about how

clear the experience of intimacy is among people. Try to determine what confusion exists in their minds. See if you can identify the *causes* of confusion, if you find disagreements as to its meaning.

2. The Intimacy Workshop

The Case of Bill and Mary—Continued

Bill and Mary had met in one of those rare but beautiful ways that people sometimes come together. After they had gone from the party, each felt empty. Each one wondered if the other felt the same way that he did. Mary felt miserable. She had the apprehensive feeling that something beautiful might just be slipping through her fingers. However, she had been raised "properly" and felt inwardly uncomfortable about taking the initiative to call him to try to reestablish their contact. Although they hadn't exchanged telephone numbers at the party, she knew it would be easy to obtain his number from a friend.

But she was stuck in the impasse! Should she wait, hoping he would call—as she was trained to do? Or should she take the initiative and risk the possibility that she might have misread his apparent interest in her? Should she take the chance that he might respond very coolly to her, or think that she was a "man-chaser"? Boy, was she stuck!

Bill too felt terrible. The memories of that rare soul-touching were still vivid. He wanted to see her again. But he was also fearful. He might have merely encountered Mary at a moment when she had a deep need to relate to someone—to anyone. She might *be feeling absolutely nothing now! Should he risk losing something very beautiful or risk having misread where she was with him and get rejected? For Bill that was a particu-*

larly tough situation, for he was extremely sensitive to rejection because of his basic underlying feelings of inadequacy. What should he do?

He called her! Just at the time when she had decided that she would take the risk and call him, he called her! The joy each one experienced at the more than positive response from the other was glorious! They made a date and flew high until they saw each other again.

Much of the previous magic was still there. "Could it be . . . ?" Each one hoped inside. After the date they went to her apartment. They talked long and late. They had the feeling they had known each other for a long time. They drew closer and closer to each other, and engaged in much more physical closeness than either one really wanted or had thought they might. As they parted, ancient anxieties arose inside them— along with some guilt feelings. Each wondered if he had "gone too far." They speculated uncomfortably about what the other person must be thinking right now. He wondered if she would think that "all he was interested in was sex," and she wondered if he would think of her as easy or a pushover who had been with many men.

The next night the relationship was again good. Again, the same thing happened to them physically. After the parting, both experienced more fears and guilt feelings. She had, however, experienced deep feelings of closeness with him. Mary knew that the experience was not all that she had wanted it to be, but she discounted the somewhat negative interpretation she might have placed upon the meaning of that experience.

Mary was a deeply religious person. Bill was only nominally related to the church. She pondered seriously whether their relationship was right or wrong. She had been doing what she had been taught she should not do. She tried to reduce the anxiety her guilt produced by telling herself that she probably wouldn't feel so badly if they got married later. She unconsciously closed her eyes to the possibility that their relationship might not lead to marriage. Logic and theology were not as sensible to her right now as her feelings for Bill. Right or wrong, that was how she felt.

Was it love or infatuation? The answer would have a lot to do with how she would process what had taken place between them. It would have a lot to do with the amount of anxiety and guilt she would experience. She had set it up this way. Time would tell, she told herself, but she surely did hope that it would hurry along and do some telling. These feelings of anxiety were very unpleasant.

Mary had a lot of questions about the meaning of the relationship and the feelings she was experiencing. Bill also had many unanswered questions. Both realized that they had miles to go with each other, and they had nagging questions and reservations about that journey. While their feelings for each other were still delightfully delicious, they could not shake some apprehensive feelings about a few minor annoyances they had with certain things about the other person. They were only dimly aware of the potential underlying incompatibilities in the relationship. They hoped that their relationship had what it would take to achieve the intimacy both wanted for themselves. The fact was that they didn't want to see any problems! Each subconsciously decided not to think about them now.

In this chapter I will try to answer various questions people ask about intimacy. As indicated earlier, we cannot hope to respond meaningfully to the kinds of questions and issues which follow until we have agreed upon a fairly acceptable definition of intimacy. This is a must in all interpersonal communication which gets through. This is what I have attempted to do with my definition of intimacy.

I do not claim that the definition I have presented is *the* correct one. But I do claim that it is a relatively concrete one on the basis of which a clearer discussion about other issues related to intimacy may be held. Thus, it is not absolutely necessary that my definition be "true" but that it be understandable. I said in chapter 1 that my concern over the use of words had to do primarily with the *experiences* behind those words. This chapter moves closer to our daily human experiences. In my practice as a psychologist, it is typical for people to share with me their felt problem and then to begin to ask questions about the meaning of their experience. In a sense, this is what I am responding to in this chapter.

What About This?

Question 1: What is an "intimate marriage"?

Is it possible to characterize a whole relationship as intimate, or do we most appropriately reserve the word for a more specific experience? My opinion is that the more specific we are in the application of the term, the clearer we will be about its meaning. To apply the term to a whole relationship is difficult to do without losing contact with its meaning.

The question, Is Bill and Mary's relationship an intimate one? is similar to such questions as Is Bill a good father? or Is Mary a good person? The questions are almost too general to permit an answer. Oh, we may glibly answer such questions with a yes or a no, but our answers would be extremely difficult to justify if we were asked why. There just are no commonly accepted criteria for helping a person evaluate whether a whole relationship can be characterized as intimate. As we have seen, it is hard enough to identify what an intimate *experience* is. No one has yet been able to identify *how many* experiences and *at what depth* these experiences must be in order for them to qualify a relationship as intimate.

If we are going to talk about an intimate relationship, I believe we should specify exactly what we mean by an intimate relationship. We should offer ways for a person to evaluate the extent to which their own relationship is intimate, and we should indicate our belief about how typical such relationships are. People want to know how on-target or off-target their own experience is compared to others. If people are constantly offered an ideal which few achieve, but their impression is that "everybody must be doing it—and we are the only ones left out," this can be absolutely devastating to them. How inadequate they might feel! They probably would feel like a failure. And since the ideal is still there—almost as an expectation—this could contribute to their seeking a divorce and trying to obtain what they think is a normal and typical experience with someone else.

I believe that if we do not know something, we should unashamedly say so, or if we are speaking of an ideal which few reach, we should also indicate this. So the answer to the question, What is an intimate marriage? is that no one knows what it is, and we do not even know the extent to which it actually exists in human experience. I believe that it *does* exist, but it is surely different for different persons. If a person *says* he has an intimate relationship, I am inclined to accept that, although I imagine that he would find it difficult to specify exactly the parameters which he is using by which to call it intimate. If he says that many people have an intimate relationship, he goes too far for me. If he says that everyone can have an intimate relationship and that they ought to, then the limits of credulity have been reached, and we have ceased communication.

I shall allude to intimate relationships in this book but only in the sense of a model—to help me communicate my points without undue additional qualifications. Behind my use of the phrase lie the reservations and cautions I have just discussed.

Question 2: Is intimacy appropriately applied to parent-child relationships?

No. At first look it would seem that we could experience intimacy with our children. But do children have the capacity for intimacy? I have chosen to limit intimacy primarily to an adult experience. Here is why. Part of my definition of intimacy, for example, is that the relationship must be purposefully selected, and children cannot be thought to have chosen the relationship in the same way at all as adults do.

I do not believe that children have the capacity to achieve the kind of intimacy I have defined. But how may we appropriately describe the relationship between parents and children? Why not simply describe the relationship as family love or parental love?

With regard to the question of whether parents and children can achieve intimacy when the children are grown, I believe it is theoretically possible that when the child achieves sufficient maturity, he could experience intimacy with a parent. However, this would require nondefensiveness, a way of managing conflict which did not hook back into old parental issues, and *mutual* self-disclosure. Few parents and children will ever let all these things happen. But it can exist.

Question 3: Can a person achieve intimacy with God?

I give an unqualified *yes* to this question! In fact, many achieve their only intimacy with God. Even those who have little capacity for human intimacy can have some intimacy with God because God is so totally adequate. Some who do not marry achieve their greatest intimacy with God. Some who are unhappily married or divorced achieve intimacy with God.

But let's keep the picture clear. The other side of the story is that many who are very happily married, who achieve much intimacy in their marriages, and who are fully functioning persons, also achieve much intimacy with God! Intimacy with God is *not* a compensatory, substitute relationship which makes up for the loss of human intimacy. It is a separate intimate experience. It exists alongside human relationships.

A God-intimate may or may not have the ability to achieve human intimacy depending upon how he sees the human relationships. On the one hand he may see humans as having so many intolerable shortcomings that they are never quite accepted by him. He may see man as basically evil and primarily in need of "saving." After salvation, his status is only improved slightly—"a sinner saved by grace." Such a person may never be able to understand and accept human weakness—a necessary prerequisite for intimacy.

On the other hand, a God-intimate may be much more capable of achieving intimacy than either an unbeliever or the God-intimate described above because he sees this person as God's handiwork, as God's special and unique being. He may feel the hand of destiny as he expresses his profound impression, "God meant us to come together." Such a feeling adds a sanctity to the relationship in a way that nothing else could ever do. He sees the other person not as "damaged merchandise" but rather as a fellow-sojourner who is "tuned to the same wavelength" in life.

Question 4: Can a person achieve intimacy without sexual relations?

The answer is yes. The most obvious illustration is intimacy with God, but there are many other human examples. Sexual relations can increase or deepen intimacy and it can also decrease it. But intimacy is possible without sex. Males can have an intimate relationship with other males (and females with females) without homosexuality being involved. Men and women can have intimate relationships with each other without sexual relationships being involved. Also, it is obvious that there is much sex that occurs without intimacy. Sex and intimacy have a "moderately positive relationship" to each other—as science would describe it.

Question 5: Can a person achieve intimacy with more than one person?

I think it is clear that potentially a person could achieve intimacy with more than one person. There is nothing in my definition to preclude that possibility. But the question becomes more complicated if we add to the question the words, "at the same time." It is even further complicated if we ask whether a person could have two *primary* intimate relationships at the same time—or more than two, all deeply intimate relationships.

I believe it is *theoretically possible* for a person to achieve intimacy in two *very important* relationships, at the *same time,* at *some depth.* The practical issue is not really whether a person has the *capacity* for such relationships but whether an individual has the necessary *energy* and has arranged his *priorities* for such an investment in human relationships.

The fact is that most people tend to have one primary relationship and one primary life interest which they pursue. Incidentally, love and work was Freud's formula for happiness. If both are pursued with vigor, there is usually very little energy left to pursue anything else. For example, people who love their work do it in their spare time too. And people who commit themselves primarily to be deeply intimate with their loved one look for extra time for the two of them to spend together.

On the other hand, people who do not like their jobs look for other ways to brighten their lives, while people who do not achieve sufficient intimacy (for them) with one person often look for other appropriate opportunities for intimacy. They may try either to add this to their present relationship, or they may look for an entirely separate relationship in which to achieve more intimacy.

The issue involved in this question is one of felt satisfaction and of the investment of energy, rather than an issue of capacity or capability. I have known of cases where a person *claimed* to be involved in two intimate relationships, but little was known about that person's investment in his life pursuit, and nothing was known about the relative depth of intimacy he was able to achieve with the two persons.

Question 6: Must intimate relationships compete with one another? Is jealousy inevitable between intimate relationships?

Most people would say that all intimate human relationships must intrinsically be competitive and, therefore, must involve jealousy. There are others, however, who contend that it is possible for an individual to have more than one intimate relationship without there being any *significant* amount of unmanageable jealousy. To me the truth of the matter is that the deeper and more intimate each of the two intimate relationships is, and the more equal the two relationships are regarding intimacy, the greater will be the competition for the time and energy of the loved one. Therefore the tendency will be greater for jealousy to exist.

There are many possible combinations of multiple relationships. There can be a primary, deeply intimate relationship, combined with a secondary, only somewhat intimate relationship. There can also be one primary and two or three secondary intimate relationships. Probably the more relationships there are, the less deep will be the intimacy in all the relationships, with the *possible* exception of the primary relationship. Yet that one too may suffer neglect due to limited time and energy if nothing else!

There can be two very primary relationships. Here is where most of the friction will occur. Even though both agree that such relationships could be noncompetitive, it is doubtful whether such a relationship can be noncompetitive or remain that way very long. We don't have good longitudinal follow-up information on such claimed relationships. My guess is that they are very short and very rare.

I know couples who purposefully encourage the other partner to seek fairly close relationships with others. This, they say, forces them to deal with the jealousy issue and other relational issues also. They say that this brings energy into their own relationship and helps them to keep working diligently on it. They seem to see the other relationships as motivating for them to work on intimacy in their primary relationship. It stimulates them to greater effort.

They say that their primary relationship is nourished by the input of the second individual with whom an intimate relationship has been established. New issues are constantly raised. Neither takes the other for granted. Interests are broadened, they say.

I notice that in such relationships there usually is a line somewhere beyond which the individual is not permitted to cross without placing great threat to and stress upon the primary relationship. Sometimes these lines are carefully discussed and agreed to in advance. Often the individuals do not discuss the threat-sensitive areas sufficiently, or they are so out of touch with their feelings that they do not know where that uncrossable line is until it has been crossed and their defensive sensitivities have been activated. They have not anticipated well or communicated fully about the possible problem areas in such a relationship.

I have not even mentioned sex, the careful reader may notice. I am *not* assuming that it is part of any of the relationships I have been discussing, except perhaps the primary one. But my guess is that it may already have been read into my discussion at some level of consciousness. If so, my earlier point in chapter 1 is strongly reinforced—that we have learned almost automatically to associate sex with intimacy, although that is not at all necessary.

Sex could be a part of nearly all the relationships I have just discussed, or it could be part of none of them. It is an added-onto ingredient—important to but not essential to intimacy!

My answer to the question is that jealousy is almost inevitable in multiple deep relationships. A great deal of energy has to be invested merely to keep *one* relationship going and alive. Jealousy, due to competitive relationships, might bring useful heat into the relationship without a dangerous fire, but it would take a lot of additional energy just to manage these jealousy issues effectively. This would place such a drain on the energy systems of most persons that few could endure this amount of stress for long. The kind of multiple intimacy relationships most likely to survive with minimal jealousy is one primary, deeply intimate relationship with sex, and several much less deeply intimate relationships with no sex.

Question 7: Can intimacy with God be destructively competitive with human relationships?

Although a first-impulse response might be a moralistic "it should not," yet the sober reality of human behavior forces upon us the conclusion that in fact it sometimes does. I know of cases where a deeply religious person chose to get married, but it was obvious that his highest commitment was to intimacy with God *alone*. The commitment was exclusionistic, leaving no room for the spouse. Sometimes this is the situation with ministers and their wives.

The relationship between this kind of minister and his wife is such that not only does their intimacy get second place but often it is a *distant* second place. The wife in this kind of marriage often is very reluctant to express her felt dissatisfaction in the early years of the marriage because—well, who could or should compete with God? However, as the years wear on and as she becomes more and more aware of the relationship she sees other couples building, she may become very restless and uncomfortable in her marriage relationship. Then as she may also begin to experience the "trials and tribulations" which sometimes occur in the ministry, she may start to feel very resentful. She may feel shortchanged and angry.

Sometimes this anger is directed at the church. She wonders if all those people are really "worth it"—"it" being her felt loss of intimacy. She may also turn her anger upon her husband and demand from him some form of compensation to make up for all her lost years. What she wants exactly she may not know, but he *will* pay! Of course this is not a healing solution because it only produces conflict. If, however, she can get rid of her anger and they work out of the conflict stage, they *may* be able to move on to intimacy—other factors being in place also.

I observed one case where the woman was so dedicated to intimacy with God that the man was only a very small part of her life. They were not in the ministry. He could not get through to her, and she felt his efforts to get in touch with her were intrusive into her relationship with God. She told him he was not spiritual enough. The problem was heightened when a child came along, and he was even more excluded. He finally asked her for a divorce, and she was more than accepting of his request. Actually, she got what she really wanted—intimacy with God, a baby to love and care for, and a divorce without guilt feelings.

And so it seems that even intimacy with God can compete with human intimate relationships. Some religious groups have attempted to make a separation between deeply intimate relationships with God and deeply intimate relationships with people. They require their clergy not to enter a deeply intimate heterosexual human relationship—marriage. Most religious groups, however, prefer to recognize the problems and to encourage couples to derive strength both from each other and from God—and to keep jealousy and competition reduced to a minimum through communication and careful contracting.

Question 8: Can an intimate relationship cease to exist as such?

Yes. We must continually work on intimacy if it is to survive. I believe that relationships which once were intimate may cease to be so, but I also believe that they can be revived again to intimacy if both parties commit themselves to the task. People *can* change! If I did not believe that, I could not believe in religious conversion nor could I be a psychotherapist. I do believe people can change—*if* they want to.

Question 9: Is counseling an intimate relationship?

Why do people come to counseling? After all, there is a certain self-humbling process a person has to go through in order to permit himself to come to counseling. First, the individual has to admit that he indeed does have a difficult problem. That's hard enough. But then he has to admit that he is not able to solve his problems by himself—at least for right now—or that he is not able to solve them quickly enough to enable him to deal with some impending crisis. This leads to the admission that he needs some outside person to help him.

But that's not all—he still has to bring himself to *say* this to another person—to his counselor. If the person coming for counseling is a Christian, that often makes it even more difficult because many Christians *wrongly* feel that with God they should be able to handle any problem. To have to admit that they do need help is like displaying a lack of faith in God or like insulting the strength of God's power to help. Some may feel that they are letting God down or being disrespectful to him by going to another person for help—even if the counselor is a Christian.

Another difficulty in going to a counselor is that the individual may find he has to explain he is going to counseling to others. It takes a lot of courage to see a counselor. I commend the personal strength of those who can give themselves permission to seek such help.

I want to say emphatically, though, that I believe going to a counselor can be of great value. When a person talks to a counselor, he is talking to one who is trained to remain objective about the individual's problems. In counseling, a person can learn how to increase the accuracy of his self-perception—to be able to be more objective about himself. He also has someone to whom to be accountable. In moments of weakness, therefore, he may be less likely to victimize himself since he knows he will *want* to confess what he is about to do to his counselor at the next session.

A person who comes for counseling has the opportunity to talk to someone who is trained to search, if necessary, for any deeper causes of a person's difficulties. He knows how to help the individual explore areas of his psychic functioning which might be too frightening for the individual to seek out on his own. Also he now has someone who offers him what unfortunately has become a fairly rare human experience today—the opportunity to be listened to, to be cared for, to feel understood, to be accepted, to be heard, and to be unjudged.

With regard to the relationship between help from God and counseling, it could be that one of God's "mysterious ways" of working is to use a Christian counselor. God works in wonderful ways not always understandable to us. Counseling may in some cases be the way an individual is helped best by God. And so I believe counseling offers many values to an individual.

If these be characteristic of this special kind of relationship, does counseling qualify as an intimate experience? Counseling may, on the surface, seem to resemble an intimate relationship in several ways. For example, people do say that they tell their counselor "intimate things" about themselves, by which they mean personal things which they tell few other people—perhaps no one else. And many clients do experience warm feelings for their counselors because they feel so deeply understood, accepted as they are, and cared for by this listening, receptive person, sometimes for the first time in their lives. For this they are grateful, and they reciprocate with warm feelings.

Some clients stay in therapy for months and even years. They sometimes find it difficult to terminate such a treasured relationship. Termination in a few such long-term situations may amount almost to a grief experience for the client. And so on the surface some may see similarities between the counseling relationship and an intimate relationship. Yet, there are important differences.

The counselor devotes only a certain restricted amount of scheduled time to the client and the client pays fees. The counselor experiences "unconditional positive regard"—as Carl Rogers calls it—for the client, but there is always a certain amount of separateness maintained in the relationship. The counselor is trained to avoid personal involvement in the relationship. This keeps him ethical and helpful, and it also permits him to be able to survive psychologically as he works in this deeply personal occupation.

The counselor does not have the same amount and kind of affection for the client that the client sometimes has for the therapist. The therapist, for example, typically does not share deeply personal things in his own life with the client, especially when it does not specifically pertain to the client's problem. However, he may share a few relevant things to help the client feel less "abnormal" and to increase the rapport in the relationship. So in several senses, there is little relative mutuality in the relationship.

If a client begins to move too close to the therapist and the latter senses that the client is attempting, at some level of consciousness, to change the nature of the relationship to something which is different from counseling, typically the therapist will immediately identify to the client what he sees might be happening. He exposes the movement and helps the client deal with the reasons for this kind of attempted change. It is done under the pyschotherapeutic rubric of *transference*.

So, although the therapeutic relationship has many surface similarities to intimacy, there are vital ways in which they differ. This pseudo-similarity accounts for the reason why many clients feel close to the therapist and consider the relationship as extremely special in their lives. Indeed it is. However, because of the built-in disjointedness in the relationship, intimacy, as I have defined it, is never achieved in the counseling relationship. If intimacy is achieved, it ceases to be counseling and becomes an ordinary human relationship. At that point, ethical boundaries have been crossed *by the therapist,* since he has responsibility of maintaining the counseling relationship. Counseling should cease and a referral should be made.

The client certainly may experience a feeling of closeness, and if there has been little or no intimacy in the life of the client, the relationship can become precious to that person. Often, however, the counseling relationship only stimulates a person's interest in, and ability to, achieve an intimate relationship with another, more appropriate person.

Question 10: What is the relationship between love and intimacy?

Love is a word which stands for a most beautiful human experience, but with regard to its ability to represent accurately and precisely a very specific human experience, it is a contaminated word. It is used with a wide range of application. The word is used all the way from: "I really do love that watch (dog, coat, view, etc.)" all the way to "I am deeply in love with you." We tend to use the word to express *our* feeling toward someone or something. *Love* is supposed to project a stronger feeling than the word *like* but we often interchange them in our daily dialogue.

Some people protect the word carefully and will only use it to designate deep feelings for another human being or for God. Others throw the word around almost promiscuously, using it to describe any positive feeling toward anything or anybody. I think the important point to emphasize is the fact that the word *love* portrays one's own individual feeling. It says nothing about what another person might be feeling for us.

Intimacy, as I have restricted its use in my definition, characterizes a *mutual* relationship. It assumes the existence of love on the part of *both* persons over a period of time. It involves a mutual commitment. The closest one might come to the meaning of intimacy by use of the word *love* is when two people agree that they are "in love." However, unless the relationship has been developed over a period of time, and a commitment has been spelled out clearly, it still would fall short of my definition of intimacy.

So I see intimacy as a more precise description of a close relationship. It depicts a higher level of relationship. Love and intimacy do have some overlapping areas, but there are definite differences.

Question 11: What is the relationship between love and infatuation?

This distinction is the commonly held distinction between what is supposed to be true and what is supposed to be false, between what is real and what is apparent. Love is supposed to be good and infatuation bad. Love is supposed to have the ability to endure, being based more upon compatible personality characteristics, whereas infatuation is supposed to be temporary, being based more upon incompatibilities.

The fact is that in the midst of a human relationship highly dominated by feeling, we are rarely able to see the incompatibilities of an infatuation experience. We let ourselves become blinded by the light. Indeed, sometimes we really do not *want* to see the incongruities which may be very obvious to others. We may prefer to enjoy the experience and then to evaluate its meaning later. In this case, we certainly do experience identifiable feelings for another person. But although we may call it love, we may yet wonder if it is really love or only infatuation. Can it last? Is it a seed or a bomb? This is where people suffer.

It takes a keen and perceptive eye to see clearly the basic nature of a given relationship while one is in the midst of it. *It is not true that love is blind!* If that were true, we would know that we do not know. The truth is that *love is a perceptual disorder* wherein we know not that we do not know—and that is the anguish!

Many a young person has asked adults, "How can you know when it is love and when it is infatuation?" To this question most adults stammer and then mutter something incomprehensible but authoritative such as, "You'll just know the real thing when it comes along." *The Neurotic's Notebook* truly says it: "No one can understand love who has not experienced infatuation. And no one can understand infatuation no matter how many times he has experienced it." [1]

Infatuation is being in love with love. It is feeling euphoric at the experience of being valued by another person who is also attractive to us. Infatuation is an after-the-fact diagnosis of an experience rather than an in-process evaluation of that experience. We do not *know* for sure if an experience is infatuation or love until considerably after we have experienced it. Infatuation is a trash-can designation for an experience that felt like it might have led to a deeper relationship and perhaps on to intimacy, but which didn't because of its irreconcilable incompatibilities. First comes the experience or the feeling of closeness; then comes the testing of the relationship in daily interaction; then comes the evaluation of the meaning of that relationship—love or infatuation. Its ability to endure at acceptable levels over time is a crucial factor in its evaluation. Time tells.

Love has the possibility of a more permanent relationship because it is based upon a stable foundation, whereas infatuation is more temporary, being based upon less stable features in the relationship.

Question 12: Can a person be intimate with another person and yet not really like him/her?

This question was put to me in a singles conference. It took the form of whether a person could be "in love" with an individual but not really like him/her. What I hear in such a question is something like this: "I really think I love this guy, but he treats me so badly that I often want to get out of the whole relationship. I have to admit that I love him—I think—but sometimes I don't think I like him. I want to leave but I can't." (Probably this last comment should be, " I *need* to leave him, but I *won't!*")

I hear this kind of complaint not only from singles but also from married persons. However, the problem married persons present usually takes a different form. Singles are often still very deeply in touch with recent remembered feelings of soul-touching or ecstasy. Married persons may not be experiencing such feelings of love at the moment. What they do experience is *attachment*. The attachment of an individual to what is very familiar to him is deceptively powerful. The more we are with a person and the more we share common experiences with that individual, the more we find ourselves investing emotionally and deeply into the relationship with that person. That is one reason why writers for youth on the topic of dating discourage "going steady."

Many times I've heard individuals say something like: "I'd leave him, but I've invested so much of my life in him, it just seems a shame to see it all go down the drain—he does have *some* good qualities!" Although love has faded, attachment persists. It confuses a person until he understands what it is and accepts it for what it is. Intimacy is incompatible with not liking a person.

My answer to the question posed then has to be a solemn *no!* We cannot be intimate with a person whom we do not like, although we may still have feelings of love or at least attachment for that person. Our loved one ought to be our *best friend* and our *most liked person*.

Question 13: What human experiences are close to intimacy?

There are some human experiences which seem to come close to intimacy, as I have defined the experience, but which fall short of qualifying as intimate for one reason or another. One example of this would be the hopes on the part of some individuals to achieve "instant intimacy" through participation in "heavy" encounter group experiences. Also typical of an aborted attempt to achieve intimacy is having a casual sexual liaison with a person.

But to be true to the facts of reality, I must add that it is obviously quite possible for an initially pseudo-intimate experience to move on to genuine intimacy if we can believe the testimony of some married persons. This would be the case with soul-touching and ecstasy, as I indicated earlier.

And so it is possible for soul-touching or an ecstatic experience—some experience somewhat distantly related to intimacy—to move on toward intimacy, but they are *not* in themselves intimacy. However, the casualties are often many among those who "experiment around" to achieve quick, deep relationships. The personal prices paid are often inordinately high for those who seek shortcuts to intimacy. The development of intimacy takes time. Such attempts, however, do indicate the thirst on the part of the people to achieve intimacy with someone as soon as they can.

Question 14: Does one marital role model have an advantage over another in facilitating intimacy?

I have long felt that the success of any marital role model is a tribute more to the couple than to the model they have chosen for themselves. Some feel more comfortable choosing the traditional, patriarchal, male leadership role model, while others feel more comfortable with the democratic or shared leadership role model. I have yet to see a seriously proposed female leadership model! For myself, I value the *contracted* role model wherein each person, being fully aware of the meaning of each of the available models and feeling fully free to choose *any* of the models he wants to, agrees that he feels most comfortable working out of a particular model. But the decision they have contracted together is open to reevaluation at any time, upon the request from one of the two.

Whenever anyone has an equal right to an opinion, then the stage is set both for growth and for conflict. There may be less open conflict in the male leadership model, but there probably will also be less growth—and there may be more *resentment!* And that seems to be the key—the amount of resentment a person feels toward his/her mate, whatever the marital role model chosen by the two! Resentment is the deadly killer of intimacy. Until resentment surfaces, is expressed, and dealt with through conflict management, there will never be room for intimacy to bloom.

My feeling then is that there is no marital role model which favors intimacy more than another. One model may favor a particular *couple* more than another model. That may be the best role for *that* couple. The reason I prefer the contracted role model is that it leaves room for all possibilities. It is not a particular model which facilitates intimacy, but rather the individuals in the relationship—however they have defined for themselves their most comfortable marital roles. It isn't what model is chosen but how much resentment is felt which has a major bearing upon the achievement of intimacy.

Marriage Intimacy

The highly conscious reader may be fully aware that I have not described intimate relationships only in terms of the marriage relationship. Can intimacy be achieved outside the marriage relationship? A reexamination of the definition will reveal that it obviously can. Such experiences would also include intimacy with God and with friends.

Then what about "intimacy in marriage"—the title of this book? What is special about marriage intimacy compared to other kinds of human intimacy? I believe that the possibilities for intimacy are keenly heightened *within* the marriage relationship! In marriage the partners live closer together, for longer periods of time, under less stress from cultural sanctions.

Marriage commitment is a deeper commitment because the couple has pledged the depth of their love toward each other by submitting their relationship to legal sanctions. For those who do not see divorce as a contingency plan for getting out of a marriage without working on the relationship, the law is no threat. It is only a threat to those who are less committed to work on the problems which may arise in the relationship. I do believe that there is a deeper level of commitment demonstrated when people marry than when they just live together.

Marriage should include sexual relations as an important part of the relationship. Sex is not necessary or helpful to the relationship in many nonmarital intimate relationships. In some cases it only complicates the relationship and interferes with the amount and kind of intimacy which might otherwise be achieved. But sexual relations is an integral part of marriage. In the Christian tradition, we associate marriage with sexual exclusivity. The partners pledge themselves to confine the deepest and most vivid expression of their love to the marriage relationship only.

In the Christian tradition the idea of marriage is also associated with a mutual commitment by the couple which is entered into with the idea of permanence. The basic commitment amounts to a personal contract to stay in the marriage when the going gets rough and to work on it; to grow and to encourage the other to grow; and to become more as two than either could be as one. In marriage there is a mutual commitment by each to nourish the other; not to do so is certainly one form of unfaithfulness. Each partner has the responsibility to help the other person feel free rather than to feel trapped.

In summary, although the intimacy that occurs in marriage is only one kind of relationship in which intimacy can exist, it is the place where most people attempt to attain intimacy and where I believe they have the best opportunity to achieve it. Some are seeking alternatives to marriage in order to experience intimacy, but the apparent rise in the actual number of such persons may seem more dramatic than it actually is. It is new—and shocking to some—but it began from a low starting point so that the actual number choosing this course, compared to the number who choose marriage, is in fact quite low. Add to this the fact that a great many who get a divorce later remarry, and it becomes convincing that most people believe marriage is the best place for intimacy to grow. I believe they are correct!

While many fail in marriage the second (and even the third, etc.) time, many yet do succeed. And as Mignon McLaughlin shrewdly observes, "If the second marriage succeeds, the first one really didn't fail" (p. 16).

Unfortunately, it is true that in many cases the first marriage has indeed become a preparation for a second, a more successful marriage. "Really to succeed" in marriage, or to be "happily married," means being able to achieve a sufficient amount of intimacy in the marriage that each mate feels such satisfaction that he has little or no need to seek for it outside the marriage. I am referring here to a heterosexual relationship, with a sexual expression involved, for certainly we also want intimacy with God and with other human beings.

We must keep in mind the wide range of individual differences in the need levels for intimacy in marriage as we evaluate the meaning of "a happy marriage." Probably for some individuals neither marriage nor any other kind of relationship would be sufficient to meet their almost insatiable needs for intimacy. We cannot evaluate marriage solely with respect to this kind of individual. How much intimacy *should* a person have in order to meet "normal" needs? The question is unanswerable! Each person must define for himself how much intimacy he needs; *his* evaluation is what counts, for *he* is the expert on himself.

What Do You Think?

1. Try to summarize briefly my answers to the fourteen questions asked in this chapter. Include the reasons for those answers.

2. If you disagree with my definition of intimacy presented in chapter 1 and were to use another definition, how would you answer the questions I have posed in chapter 2? Which of my answers would differ from the answers which would follow from this other definition?

3. Do you agree or disagree with the distinctions I made among infatuation, love, and intimacy?

4. Ask five people to tell you the difference they see between love and infatuation. Compare their answers. Look for similarities and common elements among the answers. Compare their responses to my discussion. Arrive at your own conclusion about the difference between love and infatuation.

5. If intimacy is only an adult experience, what word or phrase would you use to describe the closeness of parent-child relationships?

6. How can you keep intimacy with God from interfering with intimacy with one's mate?

7. (Discuss this question privately with your spouse.) At what point would you begin to feel uncomfortable were your spouse to have an *intimate* relationship with a person of your sex which would *not* include sexual relations? How close a relationship could you handle without experiencing such jealousy that it would be hurtful to your marriage?

8. What is your reaction to my endorsement of the contracted role model in marriage? Do you have a strong bias that one particular marital role model is best for *everyone?* If so, how does this marital role reveal itself in your marriage? What strengths does it provide? What difficulties do you experience because of it?

3. The Ingredients of Intimacy

The Case of Bill and Mary—Continued

Mary and Bill had been going together for several months. They still very much enjoyed each other's company. They believed they were in love with each other. The strong feelings they had for each other earlier were still there, although they were not quite as vivid as they used to be. "They" had decided to cool their physical relationship—to set limits upon it. Actually it was mostly Mary's decision, with which Bill went along somewhat grudgingly.

Although they talked about the meaning of a marriage relationship, they did not talk about it explicitly in terms of their relationship. However, the implication was there. They made no commitments to each other, but neither dated anyone else. It was discussed in the abstract, on a "what if" basis. Some of the minor irritations each one had been aware of in the other person were now beginning to come to the surface. At first they couldn't talk about these problems without someone feeling hurt. This was especially a problem for Bill. As the relationship developed, however, they began to bring them more and more into the open. The reaction of being hurt eventually gave way to more of a problem-solving approach. They learned to trust the other person not to want to break up the relationship merely because one felt uncomfortable about something in the other person.

One thing Mary didn't like was the fact that Bill would never show his feelings. Even in their earlier physical relations, she realized now that there had been an element of tenderness missing. He also had a tendency to want to make all of the decisions for the two of them. She felt that he thought he always had to be right. She disliked the fact that he discounted feelings and insisted that they only pay attention to logic and "the facts" in their disagreements.

Bill had his concerns too. Mary was so emotional. When she couldn't win a discussion with logic, she would "cop out" (as he saw it) by crying or accusing him of being unfeeling—all irrelevant points to the issue under discussion, he felt.

The issues they dealt with inside themselves and the unspoken questions each one held in their hearts created many doubts about the possible permanence of the relationship. Even if they did decide to marry, they held grave reservations about what kind of a relationship they might be able to have with each other. There were so many rough edges that had to be smoothed out and they knew it. Were there simply too many?

What if they put a great deal of time and energy into trying to make something permanent and beautiful out of the relationship and then it didn't work? Look at all that wasted time and energy! Would it be better just to start over with someone else? But they did *love each other! Would someone else have* less *problems or just* different *ones? What was changeable and what was not? Would they have the capacity to change? Stubborn, unrelenting questions nagged and perplexed them. Did they have the necessary personal ingredients for achieving intimacy?*

A Formula for Intimacy: Some of This and Some of That

I don't put much faith in formulas applied to human behavior in the strictest sense. I place myself on the uniqueness side of the question of whether a person is very much like all others or whether he is unique and different from all others.

I believe that we can predict the behavior of the individual best when we know the *individual* well, rather than that we can predict individual behavior best by knowing how *other* people in general behave. The more a person is consciously aware of himself, the more he will take control of himself, and he will be less predictable because he is guided by an *internal* psychological gyroscope. He is less subject to control by external events—and thus less predictable. Also, the more specific and complex the situation we are required to predict, the less accurate our predictions will be.

And so with these beliefs about the predictability of persons, on the surface it certainly would seem absurd for me to talk about applying formulas to persons. But I believe that a formula can be applied to persons in the *broadest* sense of the term— in a metaphoric or in a descriptive sense. If we confine the formula's use to description—as we do when we use a model in science—I believe it can help us communicate in general terms the forces operating within a person. But this is the only sense in which I feel comfortable in applying a formula to persons.

Formative Factors

I think it is possible to identify some of the factors influencing the achievement of intimacy in marriage. It seems to me that intimacy is a consequence and a product basically of four formative factors: (1) personal factors, (2) interpersonal factors, (3) readiness or motivational factors, and (4) skill factors. Let me elaborate briefly on what I mean by each of these factors.

Personal Factors—By personal factors in the formula for intimacy, I refer to three things basically. (a) The first is the ability of a person to know himself; to be in touch with his basic conflicts, his defenses, his goals, and his strengths and weaknesses; to be working out his self-definition, his meaning and purpose in the world—generally to be working to answer the fundamental existential questions in his life. This aspect of the personal factor has been called *congruence* by behavioral scientists. (b) By personal factors I am referring also to the ability of a person to sense accurately what is happening inside another person, to be able to intuit or to perceive what the world looks like and feels like to the other person—what behavioral scientists have called *empathy*. (c) The third aspect of the personal factor is the ability to see things as they are. It is to have good perception, to have good eyes for reality. It is the ability to size up a situation and to see it as it truly is. Behavioral scientists have called this personal ability *veridicality*.

Interpersonal Factors—By interpersonal factors in the formula for intimacy, I refer not only to the natural attraction one person has for another—to have "good vibes" or "good chemistry"—but also to the areas of human interaction where we make significant contact with other human beings. These are the spheres of life where we experience meaningful things in common with another person—what the Clinebells refer to as "facets of intimacy."[1] The interpersonal factors are equally *essential elements* in the formula for the achievement of intimacy. Thus, even though a person is congruent, has the capacity for empathic understanding of another person, and also has the ability to see things as they are, unless there is an attraction between the two persons, and several significant areas of common interest for human contact, nothing will happen. A person's capacity for intimacy then is conditioned not only by factors within him but also by transactional factors between him and his partner—the interpersonal factors.

Motivational Factors—The third set of factors are readiness or motivational factors. By this I mean that the individual must have a disposition toward *wanting* to experience feeling. Not all persons are so disposed—especially men because of their cultural training toward *things* and *ideas* rather than toward people and feelings. The individual must desire closeness and feel comfortable with it; he must not fear it. He must be willing to take down the defensive walls he may have built through the years; he must be willing to let others into his private, vulnerable, and innermost self.

He must set such a high premium upon intimacy that efforts to attain it will receive sufficient energy to permit its possibility. This means a "priorities-management decision" on his part to place intimacy *first* in his life—*if* he is serious about achieving intimacy! It may also require intensive efforts to clarify what his values really are to help him put his behavior more in line with his words. He must be willing to bring down the many possible barriers to intimacy. In short, he must truly *want* intimacy.

Skill Factors—The fourth set of factors is skill variables. By definition, they only come through practice. Primarily it is communication *in depth* which is called for here. Intimacy is a contact sport, and the contact must not be limited only to surface levels. Those who would achieve intimacy must have a tolerance for the pressures of the depths, even as deep-sea divers do. They must have such a passion for the depths that—although they cannot stay at such levels for long because of the need to surface for air and to restore energy—they desire to return to that enchanting place again and again.

Couples who would be intimate must communicate often, and sometimes long, about real things, about meaningful things, about beautiful things, about touching things, about significant things. They must become skillful at mastering the art of communication. These skill factors are so important that—even though a person is in touch with himself, although he attains psychological empathy for others, sees things as they are, has several possible areas within which intimate contact could occur, has definite feelings for another person and a willingness to make contact—if he does not know how to communicate effectively with his partner, intimacy will be stillborn.

Of course, it is rare that, given all these other factors, communication skills would be low, for all are interrelated; yet that could happen. I have discussed these factors separately, primarily to illuminate the part they play in the attainment of intimacy, but the fact is that they actually form a composite, each aspect complementing the other. None is complete within itself. Those who would attain intimacy must immerse themselves in each part.

My Formula for Intimacy

So we arrive at my formula for intimacy. I will state the formula in probability terms. I believe that the *more* a person is in touch with himself, has the capacity for empathic understanding for another person, is able to see things as they truly are, is capable of deep feeling, actually has such feelings for a particular person, has important points of contact for intimacy with that person, places a high value on intimacy in his life compared to other values, and has practiced long and hard to communicate himself authentically to another, the *greater* is the probability that the individual may attain intimacy—*if* the other person also meets the above criteria.

Now let's investigate in more detail the personal elements of the formula: congruence, empathy, and verdicality.

Congruence: Getting Me All Together

Fritz Perls once mused that we do not marry a person, but rather an ideal; and then we spend our lives trying to get that person to live up to our ideal. I have added to his observation the fact that this doesn't work—because at the same time we are trying to get the other person to fit into the model of our ideal marriage partner, the other person is also trying to get us to fit into the model of his ideal marriage partner!

It can become a healing experience when a person becomes aware of this natural tendency within him and puts an end to the fitting game. Instead, he begins to work on understanding and accepting the other person for who he is. This does not, of course, preclude the right and the need of each person to continue expressing his wants about what he would *like* for the other person to do or to become, as long as his requests are within reason and are recognized only as requests rather than demands. Since we are all capable of change, it is possible for each of us to make some changes in order to move closer to another person if the change is deemed both self-fulfilling and other-edifying.

Congruence is required to be able to be aware of this tendency within us. Until we achieve this awareness, we cannot hope to work on a real relationship with another person. How then can we work on congruence? I believe there are two basic ways by which a person works on congruence. The first amounts to what might be called *intimacy with oneself*—the ability to like oneself and to enjoy spending significant amounts of time in solitude, renewing friendship with oneself and growing in self-awareness. The second way is to learn more about oneself through significant interaction with others. This can only be discovered through *self-disclosure*.

Let's enter now the portals of one of the most important requirements for the achievement of intimacy, and penetrate deeply into its meaning, walking both its obvious main streets and perhaps its less traveled, but fully as significant, back streets. What is congruence (being in touch with one's self)?

A Rich Heritage for Congruence

The concept of congruence has a rich history. Although Carl Rogers has popularized the concept of congruence, Gordon Allport [2] has also made landmark contributions to the idea. Allport talked about congruence in connection with his discussion of the unity of personality. He described congruence as a deep personality unity which integrates other seemingly contradictory aspects of the person's behavior. For example, Joe Jones treats his wife badly, but he is most polite to other women. This seemingly contradictory behavior on the surface is explained by the fact that Joe treats all of his close friends badly but treats all others with great dignity and respect. If he were observed more closely, it would become evident that Joe also mistreats his parents and his brothers and sisters but treats his more distant relatives politely.

Allport points out that it often takes skillful clinical observation in order to perceive such unity of personality, but he is absolutely convinced that it is there, operating behind the scenes in everyone. Each person *has* a basic personality congruence or inner unity he feels, although the individual may not be consciously aware of what those unifying features are.

But Allport also points out that we should not be so naïve as to think that if we only knew the "deeper explanation" of a person's apparently contradictory behavior, we would find consistency in all areas of his life. Oh no! That would be far too simple an explanation for human behavior. Man is extremely complex; part of that complexity is the fact that he sometimes contradicts himself. Allport is saying that *more often than it first appears,* behind a person's seemingly paradoxical behavior is an explanation, an underlying, unifying value or guideline on the basis of which he behaves. It was but a short step from Allport's idea of congruence to Rogers' use of the word.

By *congruence* Carl Rogers means being in touch with oneself at different levels of personality; this produces a unity. When we are congruent, our conscious (managing) part is in touch with our unconscious (deeper) self. The implication is that when we are in touch with the deeper parts of our personalities, we are more of a unity, more congruent. And so congruence is a unifying process wherein we "get it all together."

Let's look now at two dimensions a person must work on to achieve congruence. The first is personal growth achieved by a self-reflection; the second, personal growth achieved by self-disclosure.

Self-Intimacy

Until we can achieve a comfortableness with ourselves, it is doubtful whether we can be in a place where we can be comfortable with others. We must be able to get in touch with our needs and our wants and have the ability to perceive the difference. We must be fully aware of our strengths and weaknesses. We need to be able to celebrate our strengths and to nourish those we feel are in line with our life goals. We must learn to accept our negative features or weaknesses as truly part of us and then try to identify how we might want to modify them to make them more acceptable to us. Self-intimacy is basic to the achievement of interpersonal intimacy.

Self-Disclosure

We cannot know ourselves as fully as we might until we begin to share with trusted others important parts of our innermost self. We need a mirror that speaks truth—as did the mirror of the wicked queen in the Snow White fantasy—but we need a mirror in the form of a person. Feedback is just as essential to effective human functioning as it is to the functioning of machines in our computer technology. We must be able to get a fix on our "blind side," which always lies outside our viewing.

Here a distinction should be made. If we are talking about efforts on the part of the individual to achieve congruence—a condition of self-integration, as we are here, then it is not essential that there be a condition of *mutual* self-disclosure. It is enough for the individual to disclose himself, as to a counselor or to a confessor. However, if we are speaking of an *intimate* relationship, the disclosure must be mutual.

Congruence as the Foundation

In the family-enrichment conferences I conduct, when I am presenting a miniworkshop on marriage enrichment, I explain that the rationale for such a workshop in a family enrichment meeting is that marriage enrichment is the foundation for family enrichment. (I am quick and careful to point out, however, that marriage enrichment is never a *guarantee* for family enrichment but only a foundation—the issue is far too complex to be so easily and simplistically analyzed.)

In the marriage enrichment workshops I lead, I help the participants to do some work on themselves before we get into couple issues. I explain to them that the reason we do so is that if we are to be meaningful marital partners for someone else, we must do all we can to become a well-integrated person ourselves. As youth often puts it, we must "get our heads together." Sometimes we forget the crucial importance of self-evaluation, self-growth, and self-nourishment in the process of relating meaningfully to others.

Self Last?

Among Christians, I have heard an old saying, "God first; others second; and self last." I think I understand the point that is being made in this expression. It seems to go along with what the Bible teaches about our not thinking more highly of ourselves than we ought to think (Rom. 12:3). We have been told that "Pride goeth before destruction, and a haughty spirit before a fall" (Prov. 16:18). The point is a good one if kept in focus and balanced by sound reason. However, I have seen the point accepted so unreservedly that the result was self-depletion.

Thus, I have sought to achieve some balance with this restatement of the expression: "You have heard it said, 'God first; others second; and self last'; but I say to you that if self is always last, there will be nothing left to give to others—or to God!" This seems to be in line with another well-balanced proverb I once heard: "If I am not for myself then who will be? But if I am only for myself, then what does that make me?" Jesus said, "Love thy neighbor *as thyself*" (Matt. 19:19).

So we must learn to be good *to* ourselves before we can learn to be good *for* others.

For Myself—For You!

Both Allport and Rogers agree that the more in touch we are with our deeper self, and thus the more congruent we are, the healthier we are and the more able we will be to function effectively. Also, the more in touch we are with our deeper self, the more we will be capable psychologically to get in touch with someone else. This means that the foundation for empathy is congruence. Before we can make significant, deep contact with another person, we must first have made contact with ourselves.

This concept is the basic assumption of most marriage-enrichment theories and models. Self-awareness precedes interpersonal intimacy. Before we can hope to achieve intimacy, we must truly know ourselves. Then we have a *chance* to come to know others. After congruence comes efforts at empathic understanding. Now let's look at the second major element, empathy.

Empathy

As in the case with congruence, Carl Rogers can take credit for popularizing the concept of empathy, although he did not originate the idea. Gordon Allport points out that this concept too has a rich history. According to Allport's brief review, T. Lipps first introduced the term around the turn of the century, using the German word *einfühlung,* meaning "feeling (one's self) into." [3] It was E. B. Titchener who translated the word as empathy.

A Noble History for Empathy Too

The term was first applied to sympathetic bodily identifications we experience as "we feel our self into" what others are doing. Let me illustrate the idea first by using the analogy of athletics. For example, if we were watching someone lifting weights and saw his energy focused upon his effort to lift the weight, we might find ourselves *feeling into* the experience of the weight lifter as we also tense the muscles in our bodies.

Or again, if we were watching a baseball player getting himself ready to swing at a 3-2 pitch in a crucial part of the game, we might find ourselves actually making bodily movements with the batter as he anticipates the pitch. This is the kind of identification that was first alluded to by the term *empathy*. Again, as we watch the cascading water of Niagara Falls and begin to feel the power and movement of the water, we are achieving a kind of physical empathy with something in nature.

Henry Stack Sullivan began to apply the term *empathy* to the interpersonal aspects of behavior. He pointed out that babies often seem to experience empathic feelings for what their mothers experience. For example, if a mother becomes frightened by an approaching thunderstorm, the baby might begin to experience fear—an identification with the feeling of the mother.

At this point the term meant feeling the *same* feeling as the other person—something which Rogers changed by making a careful and important distinction, which will be discussed later. Empathy should not be understood as something we experience through mere imitation. It is not that we merely imitate or duplicate the other person's behavior and then look inside ourselves to see what we experience; rather it is a psychological projection of ourselves into the experience of the other person and a consequent *understanding* of that feeling which constitutes empathy. Empathy is not purely a feeling term; there is also a strong cognitive or thinking aspect to it, which helps it take the form of what we generally call understanding.

It was Carl Rogers who added the essential missing element to the concept of empathy, which gave it its contemporary flavor. In a very striking article,[4] Rogers presented what he felt were ten characteristics which people possess whom other people experience as helpful. In this article he communicates clearly the missing ingredient in the concept of empathy. This was the idea of a kind of *separateness* from the other which accompanies the placing of oneself within the frame of reference of another person.

Strength in Separateness

Here are a few of Rogers' more poignant statements about empathy which he makes in the article. He points out first that for a person truly to be a helper, he must maintain *psychological distance* which continues to give him the sense of being truly a separate person. Without this sense of separateness an individual could easily become "emotionally involved"—that popular phrase we use for an overidentification of oneself with a person we are trying to help, with a consequent loss of perspective on the problem. Such a loss results in the crippling of the individual's capacity to be of meaningful help to the other person. Rogers puts it this way: "Can I be strong enough as a person to be separate from the others? . . . Can I be a sturdy respecter of my own feelings, my own needs, as well as his . . . ? When I can freely feel the strength of being a separate person, then I find that I can let myself go much more deeply in understanding and accepting his because I am not fearful of losing myself." [5]

Without this firm sense of separateness, a person is susceptible to the projections of his own problems into the life situation of the other person he is trying to help. He sees the problems as "just like my own problems"—a fatal fallacy! Then he often *urges* that the person deal with his problems in a way that would be satisfying to the "alleged helper." The motivation is of course not questioned, but the capacity of such an individual to help another person definitely is limited, if not destroyed. In fact, he could very easily make matters worse for the person he is honestly trying to help. Such is often the help of well-meaning, but unskilled, friends who try to counsel their friends.

But with separateness, the individual is able to feel the strength of his being a separate person, uninvolved personally with the individual he is trying to help, yet deeply involved in understanding and helping him. Thus he is not "cold and professional" but rather he has achieved the capacity for empathy. He can be warm, compassionate, and deeply understanding, but can avoid being caught up personally in the private and separate problems the individual is facing.

This then is what is meant by empathy—the capacity to feel oneself into the experience of the other person, to feel separately the things he feels, to see what it is like to view the world from the eyes of that other person, to "walk a mile in his shoes," *and yet* to remain a separate person, objective and admittedly on the outside. He can thus view the problems of the person with clarity *and* render recognizable and deeply felt help.

Of course, it is quite possible for a potential helping person to know the meaning of empathy and not to become involved emotionally with the other person, but to make a fatal interpersonal error on the opposite side. In his attempt not to become overly involved, he can become the victim of a reaction formation—a counterbalancing movement in the opposite direction. The effect is felt by others as a cold professionalism which comes through as an uncaring attitude, a lack of warmth, a mere rendering of service or a doing of one's duty. Empathy does not permit too great a distance. Closeness is essential, but a *controlled closeness.*

Sympathy, Apathy, and Empathy

In order to delineate more carefully the relational attitudes I am discussing here, I have found it helpful to make a distinction among three words in common usage. A brief word study might shed some light on their meaning. The three words are: *sympathy, empathy,* and *apathy.* The diagram below might be visually helpful to communicate my point.

```
SYM     PATHY
 A      PATHY
EM      PATHY
```

You will notice immediately that the word stem is similar—*pathy.* The stem is derived from a Greek word which means feeling. From it we get such words as pathos, pathetic, and pathological, as well as the three words above. It can be readily seen upon closer inspection that, although each of these words is defined differently, they are framed around the idea of feeling.

Sympathy denotes achievement of the *same* feeling, *syn*- being derived from a Greek word meaning "the same" or "similar." When a potential helper achieves only sympathy for a person needing help, he can expect only to have a good cry with the other person, but other than achieving a rapport— a feeling of oneness or identification—little real help is given. They achieve only a "fellowship of suffering." We must remain aware of the fact, however, that this may be exactly what *some* people need under *some* circumstances, and that is why we cannot say it does absolutely no good at all. It often does do some good, but the ability to go further lies stillborn. Such is the help of a listening friend.

The opposite of sympathy is apathy—a *lack* of feeling, *a*- meaning "away from"—in this case, away from feeling. In apathy, there is a dearth of feeling for a person, a lack of caring, a chasm between the two people. There is no meeting of minds, only two people who happen to be in physical proximity but who are missing each other in their communication in psychological space.

Finally, we return to empathy, the proverbial middle road uniting the error of overly deep feeling on the one hand, with unhealthy distance on the other, to give birth to meaningful help. *Empathy* means a *feeling into* the life of another, *em-* being derived from a Greek word meaning "into." Empathy is the basic ingredient of the helping relationship. To achieve empathy requires vigorous and continuous self-searching and self-awareness—it requires congruence! Sometimes the path to empathy lies through the deserts of solitude and self-searching and often it is a lonely quest, but the journey is worth the effort both to one's self and to those who are the benefactors of the quest.

Now, what has all this to do with intimacy and marriage? *Only everything!* If Oden is correct that empathy and congruence are essential ingredients a person must possess in order to be able to achieve intimacy, it is clear that intimacy is not easily achieved. It may be almost impossible for some, difficult for others, and not worth the effort to others. But for those who do achieve it, it is a beautiful vision! If we can believe the poets, it is well worth the effort. To have tried and to have come close may be the lot for many, but all who write about intimacy encourage a person to try it—and so do I.

Empathy, Merging Identities, and Separateness

Those who do achieve intimacy experience a kind of merging of their identities with that of another person. I say "a kind of merging" because there is a line of separateness which always must remain. One cannot find himself by losing himself in another person. We are freer to come close to another person only when we can feel the strength of our own separateness as a person.

Thus, in marriage we are more able to speak in terms of "we" and "us" *when* we are certain that the "I" and the "you" are clearly separate and definitely established entities. This is *one* reason (there are others) why the we- and us-feeling never quite develops in some marriages. Some people are never able to feel strong and separate enough in themselves as a person to feel sufficiently free to let themselves move close to the other person. They are afraid that somehow they may lose their own sense of identity. The feeling of *us* is built upon the firm foundation of the vivid feeling of *you* and *me*.

Let's look at the third aspect among the personal factors involved in the achievement of intimacy—veridicality.

Veridicality: Seeing Things as They Are

I remember a line from a movie entitled "Charley." In the movie some well-meaning scientists "experimented upon" a severely retarded adult and were able to bring his intelligence level almost up to the point of genius. Although the tragedy of the movie was his ultimate regression to his previously retarded state of mind, even more tragic was his painful awareness of his impending loss. The line which stands out in my memory occurred when he was at the height of his newly found intelligence. At that point he appeared before a large crowd of fascinated doctors who wanted to see this phenomenon. He thanked his benefactors who had helped him *see the world as it is!* He did not mention intelligence, but it was assumed that he regarded his ability to perceive the world accurately as central to his felt intelligence.

Although the ability to see things as they really are certainly is not an adequate definition of intelligence, it does seem to be one essential ingredient. It seems to me that he who would experience intimacy must see the world as it is if he is ever going to make significant contact with another person. It would seem to be an essential aspect of the requirement for intimacy that one know himself fully and that one know another person deeply. Of course, there is no way to separate veridicality from congruence or from empathy, but I do feel that it deserves a separate discussion in order for us to communicate its underlying significance.

Everybody Sees Something

Gordon Allport points out that the ability to see the world as it is, at least at minimal levels, is absolutely necessary for survival: "Unless we keep reasonably close in tune with 'reality,' we die." [6] And so we are naturally equipped with the ability to perceive reality as it is—up to a point. However, Allport stresses that since we cannot attend to everything at once, we are forced to be selective in what we perceive. Thus, we have learned to screen out unwanted, unnecessary, and interfering sensations and information, and to point our attention to the wanted, the important, and the desired sensations and information necessary to permit us to meet our needs.

The Blind Side

While this selective perception works fine in our daily functioning, the problem comes when we begin to screen out (at some level of consciousness) what is uncomfortable, painful, or hard to understand or integrate into our usual ways of viewing reality. Thus, for example, a husband can learn to screen out the messages his wife is giving him that she is growing increasingly uncomfortable in the marriage relationship. He can learn to screen out so well the information that is obvious to everyone else that he can appear to others to be extremely naïve.

Of course, the cultural proverb offers the clear explanation: There are "none so blind as those that *will* not see." Jesus himself spoke of some, who having eyes, could not see, and having ears, yet could not hear (Mark 8:18). Such an individual does not *want* to see, for the truth is far too painful. He often wouldn't know what to do with the information anyway, even if he were to let himself perceive it accurately and to accept it as true. And so we can understand how the ability to see things as they are can be interfered with by our need to avoid pain and conflict. Often we much prefer to live on in our whitewashed world with our Pollyanna perception of reality. I believe that there is a real question whether such a person, in such a state of mind, is capable *at that point* of achieving intimacy. He has become blind to himself, blind to the other person, and blind to the situation around him. His capacity for intimacy is thus shut down.

Resurrection

I do believe, though, that such a person can again find his eyes and begin to practice looking at the truth. He can learn to handle the pain that lies therein, for the rewards he will receive after the suffering are quite sufficient if they lead to intimacy. Yet, until the scales drop from the eyes, the individual will continue to stumble through his incomplete world, viewing all around him with opaque eyes. In this condition, he is not capable of intimacy.

It was Freud who first noted how this tendency (to block out the painful from our conscious awareness) worked. He painstakingly investigated what he called "repression"—the tendency to push down into the unconscious the things we are not able to handle because they are too painful. He pointed out that when this happens, these painful ideas have a tendency to come back to haunt us in disguised forms such as physical ailments which have no physical basis, depression, or anxiety.

It is obvious that repression is *one* of the basic causes for a lack of veridicality. If we cannot bear to face something psychologically, neither will we let ourselves perceive anything that will remind us of that thing. The extreme form of repression is amnesia or multiple personality, while the extreme form of the loss of veridicality is hysterical (nonphysical) blindness (what all movie and television heroes suffer from whenever they are afflicted with blindness—for they must be able to recover their sight).

In this chapter we have looked closely at only one of the four basic factors important for the development of intimacy—

the personal factor made up of congruence, empathy, and veridicality. I have attempted to describe what these elements are, what they mean, and what a person might do to work on them. In the next chapter I shall present the interpersonal factors.

What Do You Think?

1. Plan a program of personal growth designed to make yourself a more interesting person. Follow the suggestions presented in this chapter on how to work on congruence, empathy, and veridicality. Actually write the program down and share it with your intimate other.

2. Try to think of a person in your life whom you feel you could trust to be your "confessor." What keeps you from asking that person actually to become your confessor? If you can't think of *one* person to whom you would be willing to tell *everything*, could you tell all to a *composite* of three or four people so that no one person would know all, but yet among them, all about you would be known?

3. Write down five things you could do within the next month to "be good to yourself" so that you could be better for your intimate other. Share these plans with your intimate other.

4. Purchase a book on listening or communication. Read it carefully within two weeks and practice what you have learned. At the end of one month write down to share with someone special what you feel you have learned from your experiment and how you feel you are different as a result of your efforts.

5. Try to name at least five things you would really like to know about yourself which you are in doubt about. "Play like" you have a magic mirror which answers every question you ask it truthfully. Now ask the questions one at a time. After each question, you "become the mirror" and answer

the question. If you get no answer, ask yourself how you might find the answer. Could you ask for some honest feedback from a friend? Do you need to talk to a counselor? What keeps you from doing it?

4. Exercises in Intimacy

The Case of Bill and Mary—Continued

After several more months of dating and trying to deal with the various issues between them, Bill and Mary began to talk more openly about the possibility of their getting married. It was out in the open as a possibility for them. Now another disturbing awareness began to arise within Bill and Mary. They began to realize that they actually did have very different interests. They slowly began to face the fact that if they were going to build their relationship further, they would have to find many more ways of being with each other.

They didn't know what to do at first—except to air these scary facts. It was Mary who brought the topic up. At first Bill denied it. That was his way—don't talk about it and maybe it will go away. But Mary persisted and pursued Bill. That was her way—any problem could be solved if they just talked about it, even if Bill didn't want to talk about it, even if he asked for a little time to get himself ready to talk about it later.

Eventually they both agreed that they had a problem. That was a positive step. But what should they do about it? By mutual agreement they discussed their relational problem separately with friends. They read some books. Mary talked to her pastor. Mary suggested that they go to a counselor, but Bill didn't want to do that. "We can handle the problem ourselves," he said—although he wasn't quite sure just how. So they began to look for ways they could relate to each other—for more areas of mutual interest. There just had to be more than they had been able to come up with so far.

Intimacy: You May Begin

It's one thing to study intimacy and quite another to participate in it and achieve it. Most of us seem to do much better talking about intimacy than experiencing it, but the real joy lies in the experience. As a country preacher once told his congregation, "There comes a time when you gotta stop figurin' out and start figurin' in on things!" Words of wisdom!

The fact is that in many cases *we* are responsible for keeping ourselves from experiencing intimacy. We stop ourselves! One very effective way we can keep ourselves from experiencing intimacy is to spend so much time *de*scribing it that we never get around to *sub*scribe to it. It is my hope that this work will not be just one further contribution to *that!*

In helping ourselves and in helping others to achieve intimacy, we must work on very *specific* points. "Go now and become intimate" is advice from a buffoon! It is far too general. A person needs to know *specifically how* he might go about achieving it. While no one can write such a prescription, some specific ideas and possibilities would be helpful.

But we must keep in mind the fickleness of feeling. We cannot just command ourselves to experience a certain feeling. Feeling has a life of its own, arising spontaneously. Who is able to predict, direct, and otherwise control a "high feeling" (without chemicals, of course)? Feeling is independent, awesome, proud—beautiful! No, we must approach feeling with reverence and respect. We must *do* first and patiently trust that we shall be washed over with feelings of closeness after the action. If they do not come, we must look more closely at ourselves and our relationship with our potential intimate other.

In order to work on the achievement of intimacy, we will need to identify some climates, some atmospheres, some behaviors which others have found to be fruitful in helping them to become ready for intimacy. No one achieves intimacy without previous efforts to make himself ready for the experience, whether that effort is a conscious or an unconscious one.

Here I would like to suggest some specific things a person might do to create a climate in which he could achieve intimacy with his intimate or potentially intimate other. I shall use as a model or guide the areas of intimacy identified by the Clinebells—as others also have done.

The most familiar part of the Clinebells' book on *The Intimate Marriage* is the second chapter, "The Many Facets of Intimacy." [1] In that chapter the Clinebells identify what they feel to be twelve facets or dimensions of potential intimacy within marriage. What they present amounts to twelve spheres of activity or behavior within which intimacy is most likely to be observed in human interaction. The Clinebells use this model primarily to identify areas of *possible* intimacy. They do not presume that intimacy does in fact occur in all those areas in all marriages. They see them only as potentialities. I agree.

Although the Clinebells do not compare the different areas one to another with regard to their relative potential for the achievement of intimacy, they do write three of their later chapters on three of the facets—communication, sexuality, and the spiritual area. This may amount to an indirect comment on their part as to what they see to be most crucial among the twelve dimensions, although they do not say so.

While it is surely true that the value of a particular area depends upon the value *placed* upon that area by a given individual, I do believe that certain areas in themselves tend to excel in potential strength for building an intimate relationship, compared to the other areas.

As I review the list, my first reaction is that there seem to be certain areas which are almost *must* areas. They are spheres wherein, if intimacy is not achieved, the hope for the relationship is slim. For example, I believe that in nearly every marriage, unless emotional and sexual intimacy exists, even if there be closeness in several areas, intimacy will fail to rise higher than a mere wistful hope in that relationship. Some areas then are of *crucial* importance. Let me now describe and evaluate each facet of intimacy, attempting also to be very specific as I suggest ways one might achieve intimacy in a particular area, should he wish to do so. First, let's briefly survey the areas and their meanings.

A Summary of the Areas of Potential Intimacy

I have paraphrased what the Clinebells presented as areas of intimacy and have arranged them in accordance with my perception of their relative value and fruitfulness for increasing intimacy. The first three I personally do not consider to be areas in which to work but rather interpersonal skills or happenings having important bearings upon intimacy.

(a) *Communication*—the ability to hear the other person deeply and to be deeply heard

(b) *Crisis*—the closeness which arises when people suffer together

(c) *Conflict*—the preparation which must be made to be ready to experience intimacy

The fourth area—*commitment*—may be viewed in two ways. If we view it as a commitment of two people to each other, it is a necessary foundation for intimacy, and part of its definition. However, if we view it as a joint commitment a couple makes to something outside themselves, then it may be viewed as an area in which to work to enrich the atmosphere needed to produce intimacy.

1. *Commitment*—as described above, the first real area in which to work on intimacy

2. *Intellectual intimacy*—the feeling of closeness arising from the sharing of valued ideas

3. *Work intimacy*—the feeling of closeness derived from joint efforts in mutual tasks

4. *Recreational intimacy*—the feeling of closeness derived from the celebration of the mutual sharing of non-task-oriented time

5. *Creative intimacy*—the feeling of closeness arising from sharing the euphoria of creating or discovering something together—a child, a new idea, a product

6. *Esthetic intimacy*—the feeling of closeness arising from experiencing the sublime in the presence of another and sensing that it is experienced by the other person also

7. *Spiritual intimacy*—the feeling of closeness derived from the experience of God together

8. *Sexual intimacy*—the feeling of closeness derived from the fusing or merging of persons through sexuality

9. *Emotional intimacy*—the feeling of closeness arising from touching another and being touched at deep levels of feeling through sharing and self-disclosure

I have ranked these areas in the order in which I see them to be of increasing importance to the development of intimacy between two people. In placing spiritual intimacy third in importance, I am not de-emphasizing it; distinction between two people's achieving intimacy and an individual who experiences intimacy with God. I have known intimate marriages where neither were intimate with God, but I have no knowledge of a marriage being described as intimate wherein either or both were intimate with God and not intimate with each other sexually or emotionally.

Three Important Support Areas of Intimacy

There are three areas which I do not feel are work areas of intimacy, although they certainly are directly or indirectly related to it.

Communication—The Nervous System of a Relationship

Communication is obviously important in any kind of interpersonal transactions, but it is a learned skill. Unless communication means explicit *training* in communication for couples, such as exists in the Minnesota Couples Communication Program [2] or as it exists in marital therapy, it is not of the same nature as the other areas such as the spiritual, the emotional, the aesthetic, or the sexual, wherein one may work.

Communication permeates all of the areas of intimacy. It is like the neural structure of the relationship. If it is not functioning well, the couple will experience a kind of relational numbness. If it becomes very nonfunctional, a paralysis of the whole relationship may set in, or the relationship may die. And so I consider communication to be an important support to intimacy, but not as specific a "work area" as the others which follow.

Crisis—The Fellowship of Suffering

Crisis intimacy does not seem to belong with the other work areas either. Although a person may feel very close to another who is also experiencing some crisis, the feeling of closeness which arises from a crisis is not something which either of them plan; so it does not meet one of the criteria set forth in my definition of intimacy in chapter 1. One cannot *work* on crisis intimacy. Crisis intimacy arises unpredictably from an unfortunate and fortuitous set of events, with the result that one person clings to the other in order to weather a storm or to survive a tragedy; but this experience is more defensiveness and reactive than purposefully initiated and activated by the individual. The result is the same—a feeling of closeness—but the factors which give rise to the feeling are not usually those which a person would choose to occur. The feelings of closeness are undeniable and helpful. There does exist an experience we might call "crisis closeness," but I do not consider it to be intimacy. And it certainly is not a work area.

Conflict—The Storm Before the Calm

I've observed some couples who have attended a marriage enrichment retreat who, as they went through the experience, became increasingly disenchanted both with the experience and with their relationship—which is the *opposite* of what is supposed to happen in a marriage enrichment event! By the time they reached the end of the marriage enrichment experience where the emphasis of the program was on setting up the atmosphere for the experience of intimacy, they were so upset that sometimes they could not even continue; they withdrew from the experience by choosing to pass up participation in the suggested intimacy exercises. In some of these cases I had an opportunity to obtain more information about what had happened to them. Here is what I learned.

Although the retreat had been promoted as primarily an *enrichment* event designed for couples whose marriages were in a *comfortable* place and for those who wanted to make their *good marriage* even better, these few couples had come to the retreat with their marriages deeply in trouble! They were hoping (against hope) that this experience might miraculously do something for their marriage which they were unable to do by themselves. They wanted the retreat to function for them pretty much as a counseling experience. In short, they wanted inconspicuous therapy.

But they experienced the sobering truth that intimacy cannot be born until there is an adequate preparation for its birth. Before intimacy can occur, serious unresolved conflicts between the couple *must* be squarely faced, openly and honestly. The couple must settle important issues. Conflict management must precede intimacy. If one is to arrive at the celestial city on the mount of marital mellowness, he must first pass through the valley of the dragon. Some never make it through that valley! Some are too afraid to enter. But for those who successfully pass through it, they are amazed at how minimal are their wounds and scars. Scar tissue dissolves and wounds heal quickly in the healing atmosphere of the mount.

Commitment—The Borderline Area

Commitment has two possible meanings for intimacy, as I said earlier, each of which must be treated in a different way. If by commitment is meant the commitment of a couple to each other and to the concept of marriage, then I see it more as an important supportive foundation for the whole relationship. It would be similar to communication. Without it, the marriage could not survive. It is a must.

If, however, commitment is viewed as a mutual agreement by the couple—that certain values are important in marriage and life on the basis of which they form a kind of pact or bond to pursue these things actively together—then it certainly would qualify as one of the legitimate areas of intimacy in which work could be done.

The Nine Work Areas of Intimacy

1. Commitment: Finding and Agreeing on Where It's At

A couple may find intimacy by committing themselves to something they both consider to be of great value or worthy of the investment of large amounts of their time and energy. In the process of deciding what this concern shall be, the couple will have to compare their values very carefully. They will have to conduct a personal and thorough values clarification self-study to see what ranks first with them in terms of the priorities of their lives, what ranks second, and so forth. If they can agree on a few basic goals to which they will commit themselves, the pursuit of these primary values can bring them closer to each other. Daily, as they move nearer to their goals, they will feel both personal and couple growth.

Possibilities—In this section I will discuss some specific possibilities for those who would dare to grow. Of course, the list of suggestions will not be exhaustive; rather, it will be a *stimulus* to your own creativity to work in these areas. I am assuming that a couple would be extremely interested in doing some hard work on intimacy in their marriage. If not, they probably can relate well to one of the "proverbs" I found in a book called *The World's Worst Proverbs:* "He who lies on the ground cannot fall off." [3]

What are some possibilities for a mutual commitment to something outside themselves? To what kinds of things do other couples commit themselves? Some couples commit themselves to the conservation of natural resources or a life-style which consciously avoids emphasis upon material things. Others commit themselves to earn money, and some of these attach to their quest philanthropic gifts. Some put forth major efforts to produce and/or to support the creative arts. Others pursue civic goals. Some work on community improvement, and others devote themselves to the guidance of youth. Some give themselves to the nurturing of children other than their own, and others focus energy upon special kinds of children, such as the physically or mentally handicapped. Of course, many commit themselves to church work and/or to mutual careers either related to the church or not.

Evaluation—For each of the nine work areas of intimacy I will present my evaluation of that particular area's potentiality for generating intimacy, compared to the others. (At the end of the discussion of all nine areas, I have summarized my evaluations in what I have called "The Intimacy Probabilities Summary Chart.")

A couple who commits or dedicates themselves to a mutual pursuit certainly has common goals and interests, but the commitment sometimes is to such a large, nebulous, and global goal that *specific moments* of felt intimacy may not be experienced as often as the couple might hope and expect them to occur. This is not a very productive area for the achievement of intimacy, compared to the possibilities in other areas. I see mutual commitment to something outside a couple as important for welding together the relationship, but it may contribute little specifically to intimacy. I gave it a relatively low rating for the achievement of intimacy.

2. The Intellectual: Mind Your Intimacy

If a person becomes enthusiastic about an idea he has just discovered, then to share this idea is a *must!* Some people feel that they are going to explode if they cannot find someone to share what they have just found out! To hold it inside, to have no one to tell it to, or to tell it to someone who is much less than enthusiastic certainly is frustrating! So if two people can get excited together about some thought, some concept, some formulation of an idea, they *can* feel close to each other. They can rejoice together over the celebration of an idea. There is some obvious overlap with the creative area to be discussed later.

Possibilities—How might a couple work on intellectual intimacy? If the two individuals work in the same field, it is easier. If they do not and if they want intimacy in the intellectual area, each will have to learn from the other. Of course, it does not follow that if one *knows* something about a field that he, therefore, will *appreciate* it; but assuming that one can *learn* to appreciate the field of the other, then ideas can be shared with enthusiasm, resulting in a feeling closeness. If one cannot learn to appreciate the field of another, he can at least affirm the enthusiasm that the other person experiences, and he can rejoice at the euphoria of the other. This will, however, fall far short of the meaning of intellectual intimacy, for the affirmation is secondhand, long-range, and not fully mutual.

If a person cannot get interested in the work field of another, the two can look for other areas where they *do* share common intellectual interests. They can read books together and discuss them; they can watch movies and stimulating television programs together and discuss the themes they perceive in them. They could write a book together or an article for publication, or they could write and share poems or do various program designs together.

Evaluation—If all of this sounds a little dry to you, let me say that to a lot of people *it is!* There often is a missing element here, critically related to intimacy—feeling! There is a problem with the intellectual as an area of intimacy: thought is ordinarily *in opposition* to feeling. The intellectual area can only be an important arena in which intimacy may occur *if* the affective dimension is vividly present. One must at some point experience a *feeling of closeness* as a result of the joint intellectual efforts if intimacy is to be experienced. But there is yet another problem with the intellectual sphere as an area in which to experience intimacy.

One of the by-products of intellectual discussion often is the arrival at *different* conclusions about some issue. This can result not in intimacy, but rather in conflict and argument. I do not consider argument and conflict as the experience of intimacy, although it can become a *preparation* for later intimacy. It is primarily the effusive feeling of discovery and sharing that makes the intellectual area even a possibility for intimacy.

Another problem with the intellectual sphere surfaces if the two individuals have different educational levels. Intelligence is based not only upon "brain power"—or whatever we might call it (capacity, native endowment, potentiality, aptitude)—but also upon the acquisition of a certain number of facts and supervised practice at giving an intelligent appraisal of them. Education can help to accomplish these latter skills.

If two individuals have quite different levels of ability and education, it can result in a *feeling* of a great psychological distance between the two in this realm. If the intellectual area is *very* important to a person, he may feel hopeless about the fact that the other person may never be able to relate in depth in this area of life. The more important this area is to the individual, the more pain will be felt at the loss. But there is another important aspect of this matter which must be addressed in order to complete the picture. And it could be a saving point.

The two individuals can respect the *kinds* of intelligence each one excels in. Most psychologists today are convinced that intelligence is not a unidimensional aspect of personality— a single feature. We feel that IQ is a *very* inadequate, and perhaps a false, representation of intelligence. Although the data obtained by the intelligence tester during the time he is giving the test to obtain the IQ can be helpful in understanding the mental functioning of the individual, the IQ score *by itself* contributes relatively little to the comprehensive understanding of this extremely complex thing we call intelligence.

Today we see intelligence as consisting of many different kinds of abilities. It is much more realistic to speak of *intelligences* and *IQ's* when evaluating a single individual than absurdly to presume that the individual's total intelligence could ever be captured in a simplistic, single number. If a couple views intelligence as many-faceted, it becomes possible to admire and to respect a particular kind of intelligence in which an individual excels. In this case, the uninformed statement, "He (or she) is smarter than I," gives way to, "I may be somewhat more intelligent than she is in this area, but she is more intelligent than I am in that area." Without this kind of respect between a couple, there can be little possibility for any kind of intellectual intimacy. More than that, however, the marriage may be in danger because of a disrespect for a basic aspect of another's personhood.

In summary, I find the possibility for couples to experience intimacy in this area to be relatively low in the average case. I give it a low rating compared to the potentialities of other areas. But keep in mind that *in individual cases* particular couples might find some important feelings of closeness through intellectual sharing.

3. Work: Work Your Way to Intimacy

How could a couple achieve a feeling of closeness through work? At first glance it seems difficult, for work seems so task-oriented, so problem-centered, having little to do with interpersonal relations. It is difficult to see how persons and feelings are involved. Well, let's see how it might happen. Let us suppose that a couple wanted to achieve some intimacy through the work dimension. How might they approach it?

First, it would be important for the two to discuss the kinds of things that they would like to see accomplished. This would involve a process of clarification of each person's own unique values about work. Assuming that they could arrive at a satisfactory agreement about what is and what is not important in work, they would have to see how their competencies or potential competencies could dovetail to accomplish whatever projects they may have decided to work on together. Then, as all efficient workpersons do, they will have to plan carefully their work together before they begin to work their plan. This involves setting up a procedure for accomplishing the tasks and possibly the setting of target dates for the completion of various parts of the total task.

Now all of *this kind* of person-relating has the possibility of bringing the couple closer together—*assuming* they are both looking for similarities and that they are able to prepare themselves for the work relationship by previously clearing out the deadwood of their dissimilar interests. If they are honestly looking for things that they would like to accomplish together, they will have to do the following: communicate clearly; look for areas of commonality; clarify values; communicate these values to one another; set up priorities; possibly engage in skill affirmation—as one might encourage the other person that he/she does indeed possess the abilities to do some projected task; and jointly invest themselves in some venture in which they have to rely on one another. With these things accomplished, there is a reasonable expectation that some intimacy may be achieved.

Possibilities—Some specific things a couple might work on together in this area include: redecorate a room, turn an area of the yard into a beauty center, write something together, build a home, design and build a boat, a greenhouse, or some other structure; refinish furniture, begin a business, begin a valuable collection, learn to repair cars, lawnmowers, boat motors, or bicycles.

Evaluation—I do not doubt that such a mutually selected experience could produce some feelings of closeness, but compared to the other areas wherein a person could work on intimacy, the probabilities in returns are relatively low. For a special couple, yes, but for most people, probably not!

4. The Recreational Area: Play Yourselves into Harmony

I view play or recreation as a diversion either from life duties which are boring or from interesting life duties which, although they may be interesting, become tedious because of "too much of a good thing." From such responsibilities and stress we need relief in order to regenerate or recreate our psychic batteries. But we must be careful in the choice of our recreating experiences.

In some forms of play, we can relax, control, and reduce the amount of stress on us. In so doing we are being good to ourselves so that we can be a better person for others. It is easy to see that when a couple can learn to play recreatively, they increase their chances to experience new dimensions of intimacy with each other in the other areas.

Some persons have not learned how to play. They cannot

relax. They are deadly serious in their recreation and continue their high levels of need for control. They keep the pressure upon themselves turned up high. Such people find that they need to rest from their vacation. Some individuals use recreation primarily as an opportunity to release pent-up hostility which they have been unable to release in other ways. Since this is the only way they have learned to deal with their anger, it may come out in the form of the "killer instinct" in competition. These persons may confine their recreation almost exclusively to highly competitive events. In such kinds of recreation there is a serious question as to what has been freed up—the spirit or the blood pressure.

"Workaholics" are people who work unreasonably long hours and take the worry of the work home with them. But workaholism is an *attitude* underlying a behavior just as it is with alcoholism. Another person can engage in some of the same behaviors—take work home with him—but the attitude makes the difference. This individual does so because it is fun; it is recreating—especially if the work is in a creative (and thus a kind of playful) area. The difference is that he is not compulsively driven to do the work and let other important values take second place as a consequence of his compulsion. He is quite capable of putting aside his work for something else, and he does not experience guilt or rob himself of the enjoyment of the substituted activity. Although he may have a high achievement motive, he can also play and enjoy solitude. He doesn't find it incompatible or contradictory to take some of his work with him on his vacation—as potential fun.

Possibilities—A couple might begin to experience closeness through play or recreation perhaps by participating in some sport as partners or by joining together in a noncompetitive recreation such as boating, swimming, horseback riding, hiking, camping, spelunking, fishing, hunting, bird-watching, travel, studying nature, flying, or skydiving. The possibilities seem endless to the searching, creative mind.

A couple could also become spectator fans of some sport. Since we are not talking about exercise, but about intimacy, commonly enjoyed spectator-sport interests would serve to meet intimacy needs in the recreational area as well as would a participative sport. Spectator sports could combine travel with picnicking, visiting friends, and several of the above-mentioned recreational interests.

The important thing is closeness; thus, a competitive sport has some danger. It *might* be less hazardous to the relationship if the two played together as a couple *and* if they also highly respected and accepted each other's level of ability. The purpose ought to be closeness through recreational competition rather than winning and feeling superior, which is more aggressive than intimate. The cases of couples who play tennis as a team and who wind up hating each other are notorious!

Evaluation—Merely to do these things together is *not* sufficient! Only if by doing them together the couple *feels* a sense of closeness either before and/or afterward would they experience intimacy. In summary, I believe that recreation is a fairly low probability area of activity for experiencing intimacy. But it can occur, and it can also lay the foundation for the experience of intimacy achieved through some of the other areas.

5. The Creative Area: Create Your Own Intimacy

I think my subtitle for this section says it pretty well about all areas of intimacy—we must work to create it ourselves. We cannot just wait around for intimacy to fall into our laps. The way to work on intimacy is to create the atmosphere, the mood, and the circumstances which can engender spontaneous feelings of closeness in a relationship. In this section I will discuss how the creative act can foster the feeling of affinity.

I am using the word *creative* in a much broader sense than it is usually employed. By *create* I mean to bring forth things which did not exist in some particular way before. It also means to give birth to things now which otherwise would have had to wait for a long period of time before coming into existence. Thus *creativity* means the ability to perceive the most critical elements in a set of facts, to select out those elements from all the others, and to use them in an effective manner to bring about some significant result. Creativity is the bringing forth into newly unified integrations or wholes what previously were considered only separate and apparently unrelated parts.

Possibilities—I think the most obvious joint creative act between a married couple is the birth of children. One might protest here that the birth process is not creative but generative. I accept the point, but I choose to keep my use of creativity very broad. The birth process is one of the highest of human experiences. I am constantly impressed by the testimonies of women who say that their feelings at the birth of their baby were so deep that they were almost indescribable. It is a sublime experience to many. The revival of the natural methods, with the inclusion of the father as a support person in the birth process, offers even greater opportunities for feelings of closeness between the couple as they experience this special creative process.

To give life to another human being through the participative and cooperative efforts of another person stirs the heart magnificently. Then to bring to the lives of these offspring the things which one considers to be of great worth and value for their lives and to watch them respond to and assimilate these things into their very being is a deeply moving experience. If the couple participates closely in the inculcation of values, there can result a tremendous feeling of togetherness which is experienced periodically as the two proud parents observe their children and discuss their behavior. The more positive the results of these efforts, the closer the two can feel toward each other because of their parenting role.

Yet realistically it must be noted that it can also work in the other direction. If one parent has not participated fully and/or if the children begin to drift significantly from the values of their parents, opposite feelings to closeness can occur. The teenage years are often traumatic as the onslaughts of contradictory and competing value systems make their play for the souls of the youth. At this point the closeness that *can* be achieved amid such crises is vivid, even if the closeness is reactive. But it will be remembered that crisis, as with sex, can either bring a couple closer together or it can drive them farther apart. The latter can happen when one or both begin to blame the other.

The adoptive couple also can have all of these good postbirth experiences, even though they are not the biological parents. There are many ways to give birth to children other than physically. There is also the Christian concept of the new birth; there is the birth of the expansion of awareness, and so forth. The human condition of parenting does not have a corner on creativeness involving children.

There is yet another side to the issue. In my counseling I have found that some divorced parents feel that the fact they had had children was *part* of the cause of the demise of their marriage. Many secretly (sometimes openly) wish that they had *not* had children! They usually feel guilty for having such feelings, but that is indeed what they do feel. And so merely producing children does not bring closeness.

I have touched first upon the creative intimacy possible in the area of parenting because most married couples have experienced this human event, but there are many other approaches to achieving intimacy through creativity. A couple can create together the joy of the celebration of almost any event. They can create beauty through art; they can create an atmosphere, and perhaps a mood for sharing; they can create a product for giving or selling; they can create beautiful things in each other and foster the development of beautiful things in other persons too; they can perceive and create value in something previously thought to be of little or no worth; and they can create and also implement ideas. More specific examples might include: making an artistic rug together; designing and working on a rock garden; or designing and constructing an ecological home.

Evaluation—Because this area spills over into the related areas of work, play, and aesthetics, creativity is a fairly valuable arena in which to work on intimacy. I rate it relatively high.

6. The Aesthetic Area: A Touch of Class

While it is true in a sense that beauty lies within the eye of the beholder, it is also true—as we say about our test stimuli in psychology—that each object which is viewed has some amount of "pull" inherent within it. That is, although things which seem beautiful to some do not always seem beautiful to others, it is also true that most people tend to agree about what is beautiful and what is ugly.

One of the two persons in the marriage may be touched by the beauty of something; yet the other person might feel nothing, and vice versa about other perceived objects or events. Such situations of disagreement regarding beauty can produce a feeling of distance, a feeling that the two are sensitized to widely different wavelengths. On the other hand, when the two feel very much the same about the beauty of an object or event, they can feel close to each other as they experience it together.

Possibilities—A couple searching for intimacy in their relationship will look carefully for such potential beauty spots in their lives. They may love the beauty of the mountains, the lakes, the woods, the streams, the desert, or the ocean, and may make specific plans to reach such places. They may appreciate art and together tour art museums and collect art for their home. They may enjoy the beauty of a sunset and covenant to be together when the sun goes down on various occasions. They may enjoy the same kinds of beautiful music and listen to it together.

Evaluation—The arena of the aesthetic has many possibilities for intimacy, for by its nature it evokes feeling. People who are in love are touched deeply by music and the sights, sounds, and smells of the world around them. Whatever one can do to expand his own ability to appreciate more and more of the beauty of the world will bring the couple closer together. I rate the aesthetic as a productive area in which to work on intimacy. Efforts put forth in this area probably will produce rich dividends.

7. The Spiritual: The Union of Our Spirits

Those of us who identify ourselves as Christians feel that our experience with God is *the* ultimate intimate relationship. When a Christian marries another Christian who also believes this, there usually is little conflict between the relationship each one has to God and the relationship they have to each other in the marriage. Each person is fully respectful of the way the other person worships God. They can enjoy each other fully and relate meaningfully to God also.

Many couples find that relating to God together as a couple heightens their spiritual experience. We need to leave room for those couples, however, who prefer to relate to God privately in an atmosphere of mutual respect for the private worshiping by the other. Such couples will also have much to share, should they choose to do so.

In my counseling, I have observed that conflicts can occur between couples in the spiritual area. One problem area is sexual relations. A question sometimes is raised as to what kinds and frequency rates of sexual activity are "normal" or "correct." The implication is that sexual behavior inherently has a right and wrong dimension intrinsic to it. Such a question implies that some things are decent and other things indecent, excessive, perverted, or unnatural. When a person says he doesn't want to engage in some kind of sexual behavior because "God wouldn't approve of it" or that it is "wrong" (for religious reasons), then that definitely affects intimacy in two *very* strategic areas—sexual and the spiritual.

My suggestion is that if a person does not feel comfortable to participate in certain sexual behaviors, he will say so but confine his reasons to the nonspiritual realm. If it is wrong for religious reasons, it is also wrong for *practical* reasons. Focus upon what those practical reasons are. God only wills our good.

However, I would like to emphasize that the sexual problems indicated above seem to be no more typical of the deeply religious person than it is of the nonreligious or of the nominally religious person. These problems seem to be more a function of the sexual training (or lack of it) in our culture. Since deeply religious people, however, tend to refer all their experiences, including their problems, to the spiritual frame of reference, they also tend to attribute their reasons for not wanting to participate in some suggested type or frequency level of sexual activity to religious scruples. Other couples have the same kinds of problems, but they may discuss them in some other context than a spiritual one.

Another area of conflict I have discovered with intimacy in the spiritual realm is the question of how much energy a person should devote to the development of intimacy in the marriage relationship, compared to the amount of time he feels he should devote to the work of his church and to private worship. This is a very typical problem facing minister's wives.

The energy problem can present a definite competition to the relationship. I have heard distressed wives of ministers say, after many years of willingly deferring their personal and family needs to the needs of the church, "I know this is a terrible thing to say, but I honestly have to confess that sometimes I find myself almost hating my church for what it has done to our marriage and to our family. The church for me has been like another woman competing with me for my husband. How do I fight that? I can't; I just have to sit there and take it—*and resent it!*"

This kind of statement reflects the intensity of many years of frustration, but the real point of issue is the husband's priorities. Yet the wife also bears equal responsibility! She has permitted this situation to exist over the years without demanding a confrontive discussion about priorities in the marriage.

And so there are some cases where common interests in the spiritual may lead to the opposite of intimacy. I have consistently stressed the point that there is nothing intimate *in itself* about a particular area of relationship. An area with strong potentialities for intimacy has power to engender intimacy only when it fits the personalities of the couple and when it is seriously worked on by both of them. This point applies equally to this area of spiritual relationship. Now, in what ways can a couple experience intimacy in the spiritual area?

Possibilities—The two can invest themselves together in the work of a church or in some special mission or task within a church. They can grow together in the wisdom of the Scriptures through study and meditation. They can pray together and share their spiritual feelings and awarenesses with one another. They can share their perception of God's reality as it is revealed to them in all areas of life. They can search together for what is "God's will" for *their own lives*—not for the life of the other person! They can invest themselves in the spiritual growth of others and can attempt to pass their spiritual orientation on to their children. They can relate the problem areas of their lives to the spiritual and can explore together such possibly troubling areas as: sexuality, the accumulation and use of wealth, the use of time and energy, the expansion of self-awareness, the nurturing of the desire to care for others, the expansion of one's acceptance of other human beings, and many other similar life concerns.

Evaluation—Gordon Allport feels that the religious sentiment is the widest, most all-encompassing sphere of human functioning, for the religious person must integrate into one reality *all* known facts.[4] This area of involvement may require more of a person than all other areas of human behavior, but the payoff is also greater. This is probably true as it applies to the spiritual realm of intimacy. I rate this area of intimacy high. It has a welding power that goes deep—to the farthest reaches of the soul. It may have the greatest potentiality of all to foster intimacy for nonmarital relationships.

8. The Sexual Area: Something in the Way He/She Moves Me

I once saw a plaque in a restaurant: "Money isn't everything, but it's way ahead of whatever is second." I think many people feel this way about sex as it applies to human relationships. You will see that I have placed sex high among the areas of potentiality for intimacy. I see sex as being much like the way industrial psychologists view money as a motivator to working people—it is never found in the first position on the various self-report lists obtained by those who study work and motivation, but it's on everyone's list and is always among the top motivators.

Possibilities—What can a couple do in the area of sexuality to cause deeper intimacy? First, each person can make sure that the other person feels that his sexuality is fully accepted as valuable and good. The two can embrace the attitude that human sexuality is a gift from God and is therefore good and wholesome. It is not a necessary evil and should not be thought of as such. It is rather a special way to offer a most vivid and beautiful expression of one's love. As such, it is not merely an outlet for tension reduction; nor is it merely a duty that anyone is obligated to perform (it's not a performance either).

The couple can plan as necessary to make sure that a sufficient number of sexual experiences occur to satisfy both persons. They can communicate openly their sexual wants *as spe-*

cifically as possible by indicating exactly what is pleasing and what is discomforting. They can keep an open mind for experimentation and be alert for unplanned-for, spontaneous sexual experiences. They can work on making sure that the time immediately preceding at least some sexual experiences is warm and unrushed. They can remain close to each other after their experience. They can affirm the meeting of their sexual wants by their mate with praise.

They can work on their bodies to keep them as clean and as attractive as possible. They can learn to deal with conflicts at times other than during or near their sexual experiences in order to avoid negative feelings becoming associated with their sexual relations. They can learn through reading and communication how their own bodies function and how the body of their spouse functions.

Evaluation—Sexuality is an extremely important sphere within which intimacy can occur. Sex is a sharpener or an intensifier of experience. It can deepen an already intimate relationship, but it can also embitter a person who finds himself in a bad relationship. Sex in this latter situation only makes things worse. But other things being good, sex is among the most valued of human experiences; thus, it can help build intimacy. Sexual relations is what differentiates marital from nonmarital relationships in the Christian tradition. It is supposed to be special.

And so, sex *is* highly important for human intimacy. There may be a *very few* situations where marriages can remain vital and intact without sexual relationships (as in the case of individuals who may have been devastated by accident or disease and who may have been able to compensate through the emotional and other areas). But these marriages are rare, I believe. Typically, when sex leaves the field, so does intimacy, and most of the time, so does the marriage. I rate the sexual area as of vast significance for intimacy in marriage and as irrelevant to other kinds of intimacy.

9. The Emotional Area: Close to You

In one sense emotion is like communication—it is a means by which intimacy is experienced. However, unlike communication, it is the core of the definition of intimacy—feeling. There can be communication between two people without feeling, although the communication will only be partial and fragmentary. But there cannot be mutual feeling between two people without communication, verbal or nonverbal. Therefore, I see feeling or emotion as a legitimate area on which to work to experience intimacy—through communication.

One can experience a feeling of closeness at different levels. Perhaps the most typical feeling of intimacy is the quiet, warm feeling of closeness derived from a thousand previous close encounters. This feeling isn't as vivid as other feelings of intimacy, but it is no less valid. Often it is expressed in an unhurried, admiring gaze into the eyes of the intimate other, accompanied perhaps by gentle touching and a sensing that all is well. The verbal or nonverbal message is transmitted: "I love you." "I deeply respect you." "I am deeply touched by the fact that you love me." "I'm glad you are with me."

There is also a more desperate feeling of closeness which is experienced by those who are filled with the realization that they almost lost something precious and beautiful and that it was only barely saved at the last minute. This feeling typically occurs after a nearly tragic accident, a nearly fatal disease, or a mistakenly chosen separation from a loved one. This feeling of closeness often is expressed by the individual's holding onto the other with an almost crushing squeeze and with great feelings of cherishing. It is as if one were saying, "I'll never let you get that far away from me again."

Perhaps the most vivid feeling of closeness is the first realization in a given relationship that one is loved in return. To love is beautiful, but often painful until the moment when a person realizes he too is loved in return. Then the feeling turns into an incomparable euphoric high. One comes down delightfully and slowly from such heights, for the atmosphere up there is benignly intoxicating. This often is what happens in first love or at the first of a new love. The longer it is between loves, the more vivid the feeling sometimes is. The feeling is glorious, but it will not qualify for true intimacy until it has been refined in the fires of conflict and stabilized in the cool, tempering waters of open communication.

Another kind of quiet closeness is the placid feeling of the rightness of being together at a given time or place and an accompanying feeling that it would not be appropriate for anyone other than the loved one to be there with you. It is the feeling of fitting, of compatibility, of enmeshing, of fusion. The feeling, of course, derives from the attachment the person experiences for another, but this attachment is accompanied by the impression that the feeling could be attached to no other. Whether it could be is not the issue. The feeling is that it is so—and thus for that person it is!

Possibilities—What can a couple do to experience intimacy within the emotional realm? First, they must make every effort to work on as many of the other areas as possible—but there is more. They must become transparent to the other. They must learn to open up and disclose the innermost core of their being to the other. They must be willing to experience emotions in the presence of the other and also to share the meaning of their feelings. There must be few or no secrets between the two. They must learn to trust the other sufficiently to become vulnerable to the other—to believe that when they do, they will not be threatened or hurt, but nourished and cherished even more.

In summary, be on the lookout for the expression of feeling in the other person. When appropriate, reflect back to the other person what you think you see. Ask for verification. Learn to get in touch with your own feelings and practice communicating them without shame. Insist on the right to have your feelings heard and accepted and insist that the other person generally share his feelings—when that person is ready to do so. Feelings cannot be *extracted* from another. If the attempt is made, it is experienced as an invasion of privacy. There is a fine line here, but sharing of feeling must be the general rule.

Evaluation—I rate the emotional area as the highest among all the other areas, a jewel of great price, much to be sought after.

Let's Put It All Together

I have discussed several of the dimensions wherein intimacy might take place. These areas seem to have received at least a limited consensual validation from various writers as to their legitimacy as areas for intimacy. Now, how do each of the areas relate to one another? No one has yet attempted to evaluate and compare the various dimensions with regard to their relative potentiality for fostering intimacy in a relationship. I have tried to evaluate each of the areas as I discussed them. Now I want to compare each of the areas to the others. I have drawn up a chart which briefly summarizes my perception of the relative merits of each area as it applies to intimacy. Let me hasten to add, however, that *in the individual case,* an area which I give relatively little weight to—as it applies to the group—in general—could mean *very* much for the achievement of intimacy to a particular couple. Therefore, my remarks must be understood in the context of this reservation. I've tried to communicate as specifically as possible, even to the extent of assigning each area my *guessed* "weight," indicating that area's relative potential for enhancing intimacy.

Implications

Now what are the implications of this analysis? I see some areas as of *critical* importance to a marriage while the loss of others might be fairly inconsequential. A marriage could

The Intimacy Probabilities Summary Chart

	Intimacy Area Considered	Importance for Intimacy	Estimated Weight Factor	Evaluation of Each Area
1.	Communication	Crucial	—	Not an area of intimacy in itself, but intimacy cannot exist without it.
2.	Conflict	Necessary Beforehand	—	The necessary preparation one must make before intimacy can occur.
3.	Crisis	Possible but Not Necessary	—	Occurs by chance and evokes a reactive response which may result in intimacy.
4.	Commitment	Minimal	.5	Commitment to each other is a necessary foundation for intimacy; mutual commitment to a goal may yield some intimacy.
5.	Intellectual	Minimal	.5	Emphasizes thought, the reciprocal of feeling; may yield intimacy to a few.
6.	Work	Minimal	.5	Thing or project oriented; a few may find intimacy in this area.
7.	Recreational	Of Some Value	1.0	Activity oriented, but infused with feeling. May yield some intimacy if attitudes are playful and positive.

8.	Creative	Fairly Valuable	1.5	Production oriented, but can include people; overlaps many of the other areas; fair potential for intimacy.
9.	Aesthetic	Very Valuable	3.5	Definitely connected to feeling, although outwardly oriented; very conducive to intimacy.
10.	Spiritual	Extremely Valuable	4.0	Deeply connected to feeling; oriented inwardly, outwardly, and interpersonally; incorporates the aesthetic; infuses all other areas with meaning; engenders deep feelings of closeness to others.
11.	Sexual	Crucial or Irrelevant	4.5	Interpreted by many as closest to the innermost, and as thus perceived (falsely), extremely important; crucial for marital intimacy; not important for other areas of intimacy; other oriented.
12.	Emotional	Crucial and Irreplaceable	5.0	Other oriented; the core of intimacy; without this, no amount of compensation in any or all other areas is sufficient; this area can compensate for losses in several areas.

yet be quite intimate, for example, even with the loss of the intellectual and the work areas. It could be intimate without a significant commitment to something outside themselves if other areas remain intact. The loss of the recreational and the creative areas would require some compensation in the remaining areas, but intimacy might yet be preserved.

However, with the loss of the aesthetic and/or the spiritual, the life of intimacy would be seriously threatened if not permanently crippled. Notice that my weighting factors jump considerably when we move from the creative to the aesthetic area. The loss of the sexual and/or the emotional areas would simply be disastrous for the possibility of the survival of intimacy—perhaps the marriage!

Another impression I have is that the areas differ with respect to *how* one person relates to the other while working on intimacy in a given area. Let me employ fantasy to illustrate my point. With regard to emotional and sexual intimacy, I envision in my fantasy two persons standing *facing each other*, looking longingly at and seeing deeply into each other, wanting to cross over the uncrossable chasm which lies between them and feeling the bittersweet pain of the unchangeable distance.

With the spiritual and aesthetic areas of intimacy, my fantasy is of two people standing side by side, arm in arm, *looking outward* together toward the indescribable sunset of ultimate reality and sublime beauty. With the creative and recreational areas, I see the couple *standing only slightly apart,* working on or playing with something together, their eyes on the object upon which they are working or playing, not touching but with definite smiles of contentment upon their faces. Occasionally, they glance over at each other, reach out to touch each other or to embrace, and then go back to their efforts.

For work and intellectual intimacy, I see the couple intensely working on or analyzing something *in the presence of each other,* perhaps even with their backs toward each other, frowns of deep study upon their faces, little or no attention paid to the other, and then these efforts finally consummated by the joys of victory or by the consolations of defeat and the nobility of effort. I see admiration and respect for each other in their eyes, and I sense a feeling of pride in the work association and the relationship. With regard to commitment, I see finally a couple committed to a concept—a goal, an ideal—*standing or marching resolutely side by side,* shoulder to shoulder, faces etched with determination and jaws set. Occasionally they look toward each other with a slight and knowing smile, and then they resume their mission. These are my fantasies of the relational quality inherent in each of the areas of intimacy.

It is obvious that each of the areas of intimacy has the potential for increasing closeness and for increasing distance. For example, distance would be increased if there were: different commitments to different and contradictory goals; workaholism; competition in the intellectual, recreative, or creative areas; highly different aesthetic tastes; excessively rigid, exclusionistic religious beliefs; dissatisfaction with sexual relations; and/or emotional sterility.

Intimacy and Distance: A Delicate Balance

It is quite possible for two persons to experience intimacy with each other at some geographical distance when previously there has been an intimate relationship between the two. But it is unlikely that intimacy can be maintained for any significant length of time without a fairly deep and continued contact of some kind. Intimacy can ride the waves of distance for a while, but unless there is a new impetus at least occasionally, the surfboard of intimacy will become submerged in the stagnant waters of distance.

There is one aspect of separateness, however, which is a different matter—what has been called "distancing." There is a proverb which says, "Absence makes the heart grow fonder"; but there is a counter-proverb (which often is the case—to cover all possible circumstances I suppose) which says, "Out of sight, out of mind." The truth probably lies somewhere between these two—perhaps that absence influences the heart and mind in important ways.

There are various ways a couple might come together after being apart for any length of time. First, if the husband was away, what was his experience while he was gone? Was it fulfilling and growth producing, or was he under great stress and pressure? Second, to what situation at home is he returning? Is the house in an uproar? Is the wife in the middle of something important she must do? Third, what was her experience like while he was gone? Was she fulfilled in her activities or did she feel stuck at home in an uncomfortable situation and under stress?

If his time apart was good and he expects to feel welcomed when he returns, he may return home joyfully and full of the hope of a good coming together again. If she had a fulfilling time while he was gone, and knows that he has probably missed her, she will welcome the homecoming. But should either of these not be the case, the coming together could be disappointing and quite a letdown.

Absence or distancing can be a nourishing aspect of the relationship *assuming* that each individual experiences something good during the absence and was able to avoid experiencing anything that would accumulate resentment toward the other person. If one had a good time, and this is known by the other person who did not have a good time, resentment is likely to occur. And so absence makes the heart grow fonder *if* both parties needed the solitude, received what they needed when apart, and then were ready to reexperience each other.

Each should help the other enjoy the times apart. But each person should take responsibility for himself to enjoy himself. *No other person is responsible for making us happy!* Each of us is responsible for making ourselves happy. Certain persons and certain situations help us to do that, however. Couples should plan times apart to avoid that smothered feeling and to enjoy the coming together time!

Intimacy and Time Together

In marriage counseling, occasionally I will hear a conflicted couple say that each has "entirely different interests"—that neither one enjoys doing *anything* the other person likes to do! *If* this be true, that couple is obviously in a bad place, for they feel a great gulf between them. They feel very separate and very much "other." There is real danger for this couple. They have no areas in which to work on intimacy—*if* this indeed be the case.

However, I often find that such couples actually are just looking for some credible reasons *not* to stay together. To have a total lack of similar interests seems to be a convenient way out. When such a problem is presented to me as *the* problem of the marriage, I might need to go along with their presented problem for a while and help them initially look for ways to establish a counseling beachhead in the relationship. But when the right time comes along, I will help them focus their attention on the probable real issue in the marriage—their fractured relationship and its present meaning to them.

Most couples who are sincerely looking for help may present the problem more like this: "We don't seem to have many things in common. There just aren't many things we enjoy doing together." Such couples are honestly searching for a way to stay together and to enrich their marriage. In this case I try to help them look at the many ways they have of being together. This chapter derives partly from my work with such couples.

When I work with couples who present this kind of problem, I show them a model I have designed to help them see their problem more clearly and to begin some actual problem solving. I call it the Five Fingers Analysis. I propose to the couple five different ways of being in a marriage. I use the fingers and thumb of a person's hand as my visual model. This is roughly how it goes.

Let the thumb represent the things she likes to do, either by herself or with friends other than her partner, and let the little finger represent those activities he prefers doing either alone or with his friends. Next, let the index finger represent those things she likes to have him do with her, because she doesn't like to do them alone or with other friends, but these are things he really doesn't have that much interest in doing. He will, however, do them with her because she wants him to and because it does give him an opportunity to be with her. In the same way, let the ring finger represent these same things for him—the activities he would like to do with her company although she doesn't really care much at all for those activities. The middle finger represents those activities they both actually prefer doing with each other, and which they definitely enjoy.

I then point out to the couple that the ideal of the model is that there would be some activities for each of the areas and a large amount in the center. There should be something for themselves, something for the other, and something for the both of them together. This model provides a quick way to help them analyze the different ways they actually are together, and it helps them to identify the areas where they need to do some additional work.

Clinically, what I find is that the woman often has considerable difficulty giving herself permission to do things for herself or with her friends. I also find that many times the man has difficulty in doing things with her that she likes to do but that he doesn't particularly like to do. In these cases I point out (to the woman) that we are better for others when we are good to ourselves, and (to the man) that when we accompany the partner on activities that the other enjoys, sometimes a mutual interest can be *developed* which may be a pleasant surprise to the individual. As a result, this activity sometimes moves into the center area representing those things they both enjoy. The one indispensable area both really need to work on in being together, then, is the center one because it has the highest payoff.

In this chapter much space has been devoted to specific ways couples can work on intimacy so that a lack of information—ideas, facts, possibilities—will not stand in the way of a person's seeking and achieving intimacy. If a person fails to achieve intimacy, with such knowledge at hand, it *must* be that he does not *want* it—and he must learn to face *that!*

What Do You Think?

1. Look again at the nine work areas of intimacy and do one of the following:

a. If done by yourself, rate yourself on each of the nine areas with respect to how much *actual* experience or *promise* of the experience of intimacy each area holds for *you*, given *your* personality and interests. Let 3 mean: you actually have had good experiences of intimacy in this area or you see good possibilities for it. Let 2 mean: only some experience or only a fair possibility. Let 1 mean: little or no actual experience in the area and little value in it for you. This exercise will help you to identify your "profile of possibilities" for the experience of intimacy.

b. If you do this with your intimate other, privately rate yourself first and then rate your partner as you see him/her. Have your partner rate himself/herself privately and then rate you. Exchange papers and look at the results together. Look for similarities, differences, and discrepancies between how one person sees the other and how that person sees himself. Try to understand why discrepancies exist.

2. Take any one of the nine work areas and look at the suggestions for working on that area in the section entitled

"Possibilities." Then try to think of as many more possibilities for working on intimacy in that section as you can. You can do this with your intimate other, by yourself, or in a group. It would be particularly valuable for a group to brainstorm together on each of the nine work areas. This would produce a large number of ideas for everyone to look at and to choose from for themselves.

3. Look at the Intimacy Probabilities Summary Chart. Check out the points of contact you feel you have in your relationship with your intimate other and see where they fall on the chart. Note the weight given to the areas of contact you two have in common. Notice that the higher the weighting, the greater potential contribution that area might tend to make toward an intimate relationship, according to my hypothesis. Do your points of contact have high or low weights? The lower the weights, the more intensely one must work in that area and the more that area needs to be supported by other areas. If there are little or no points of contact in the four highest areas, it is more difficult it is for intimacy to exist in a relationship. Perhaps such an analysis will help you identify where you *need* to work as well as where it is easiest for you to work because of the natural common interests and values you have.

4. Do together the Five Finger Analysis of ways of being together discussed in this chapter.

5. How Often Is Intimacy Achieved?

The Case of Bill and Mary—Concluded

Mary and Bill found areas of mutual interest and began to cultivate them. They did a lot more to prepare themselves for marriage than most other couples do because they wanted a good marriage. They committed themselves to each other and to the relationship. They did not want the same kind of dull marriage that they feared too many other couples had. Theirs was going to be something extra special! *They would have an* intimate *marriage.*

They had informed themselves on sexuality. While they had not "checked out" their newly acquired knowledge, each felt much more comfortable about his sexuality. They were optimistic about having a mutually satisfying sexual relationship in their marriage when that time came. In fact, even Bill was now getting into the idea of saving the sexual relationship until the marriage. It was something special to look forward to, he now believed. Of course, he had his moments of relapse. Occasionally he wanted to chuck the whole idea of waiting. At times he wanted to do what he felt like doing right then. But she helped him when that feeling came over him.

The fact was that Mary too had her moments of weakness. At times, waiting to have sex didn't sound as exciting to her as she had remembered when they agreed to wait. Fortunately, Bill was in a good place on those occasions and reminded her that she might not really want that for them right then. So, between strength and circumstances they made it to marriage without having sexual relations.

They married. They were correct that the sexual relationship was as good as they thought it would be. It seemed to become even better with passing time. They really felt close to each other. Sex brought them even closer. After several months of married life they knew they had done the right thing to marry. They loved each other deeply. Bill was already in a career and Mary was pursuing one through education.

Bill and Mary talked about having children and agreed that they wanted to have children while they were young. They felt that the extra preparations they had made for marriage had enabled them to know each other so well that to have children would not at all interfere with their relationship. Children might in fact strengthen their relationship, they believed. Mary decided to postpone the rest of her education for the time being and to begin their family. They had their first child about two years after they married.

The years rolled on. Bill moved up higher in his career, obtaining more education along the way. Mary assumed primary responsibility for the raising of the three children, but she also continued her education. Seven years into the marriage she received her degree, but it wasn't until ten years into the marriage that she was able to begin work in her career field. They made the necessary arrangements to care for the children properly while they both worked.

All this time they maintained a caring and congenial relationship. Each genuinely liked and respected the other person. Their relationship was compatible. Bill passed his thirty-fifth birthday as they entered the tenth year of their marriage. Mary was thirty-three. This was the situation when the crisis came. It came in the form of a growing awareness on the part of both of them, but it remained at the unconscious level. Neither one talked about it. But an apprehension grew slowly in each of them that the marriage was drifting. It was a scary idea, and so it was regularly put out of conscious awareness and buried.

Which one first became consciously aware of the commonplace condition their marriage had come to is not important. Both knew. Finally, with deep disappointment, they openly admitted that the very thing they had promised themselves would never occur in their marriage had in fact taken place. The deep feelings of closeness, so common to them in the early years of their marriage, had now ceased to exist or it existed in a different manner. They could not tell. But whatever was different was not attractive to them.

Each said they "loved" the other—whatever that meant now (they were so confused). But each admitted that the feelings they used to have for each other were either different or they were not there anymore. They were stunned both at what had happened and how *it had happened—just an imperceptible drift in their relationship! They had let themselves become caught up in many other matters which also were important to them. While these pursuits were not really intrinsically incompatible with intimacy, they did take up the time and energy which once had been reserved to work on intimacy. And so it was clear to them what had happened: they had failed to* nourish *intimacy in their relationship; consequently, intimacy had withered on the vine which once was so vigorous and green.*

Bill and Mary cared for each other no less than before and were highly invested in each other in many ways. They liked the style of life each one led. Divorce just didn't seem relevant to the problem—at least at this point. The issue was what they wanted to do about intimacy in their relationship. Of course, what they decided to do had everything to do with the future of their marriage—whether they could stay together in a nonintimate relationship—but the focus now was upon the present.

As they talked longer and ever more intensely, the issues opened up to them more clearly. They agreed that they thought they had a foundation upon which to rebuild intimacy into their marriage if they really wanted to. As the discussions continued, they began to feel that something could be done. But they were not blind to the fact that it would require much time and energy. Were they really willing to work that hard on intimacy in their marriage? Would the payoff be worth the large investment? Their heads responded with yes, but their hearts were full of doubt. They had become so comfortable in their present life-style. Were they just too comfortable to want to change? Could they—no, would they—change, even for the hope of intimacy? They wondered what they really would do. Their behavior *would give the answer—not their words!*

How Many Achieve Intimacy?

This chapter addresses the question of how many people are experiencing intimacy on a fairly regular basis in their marriage. The answer will be pivotal to many people. The question is similar to what many of my clients ask me when they come to counseling, "Doc, is what I am going through normal? Do many people have this problem?"

People ask this question and want such feedback, not always because they want to solve their problem but because they want to get some help with their *attitude* about their problem. In most cases, I can give them assurance that many others face the same kinds of problems in their lives, and they generally feel a little better about their predicament. It helps them to know that they are not the only ones having such a difficulty. It also gives them hope if they learn that others have overcome similar problems. (They also may find some possible relief in knowing that I have dealt—sometimes successfully—with people who have similar problems.)

A couple may feel that they are not experiencing a sufficient amount of intimacy in their marriage, and they may wonder what this means. If they can also learn that many other couples experience the same kind of problem, they may feel less badly about it (because they feel a little more normal). As a result, they may be more able to work on the development of intimacy in their marriage because they don't have to spend so much time and energy brooding about how abnormal they might be.

This kind of information about how other couples experience intimacy is invaluable to them. Most couples profess to have a great desire to achieve intimacy. It would be a mistake to assume that just because they value it and say they want it it is, therefore, a rather common occurrence in their marriage. In many, many cases it is *not!*

The Professed Thirst for Intimacy

There seems to be no question that most individuals *say* they want a great deal of intimacy. Yet many seem to have developed efficient strategies that hinder them from actually experiencing intimacy. Nearly everyone professes to want intimacy and many claim to suffer severe pain if they do not feel they are experiencing it.

The careful observer of the "canned fantasies" offered by the commercializers of feeling to the television viewing audience cannot fail to pick up the direct attempt on the part of the media to market very personal experiences of people, ranging from the incidental to the intimate. The viewers eat it up! There must be *something* of felt value there for people to respond so clearly to these kinds of offerings.

I believe this kind of viewer response represents, at least partially, the thirst for intimacy we are talking about. People want to feel their way into the lives of others—at least at a safe distance. This kind of response to TV sagas cannot be explained away easily by the mere simplistic write-off diagnosis of vicarious voyeurism. No, I think it represents something more. It may reflect a wistful, dimmed awareness of the deep human need for intimacy, stifled by the achievement orientation of our culture, beaten down by the suspicion and hostility of our competitive way of life, drowned out by the noise our technology has produced, and blended into indiscernable static as it is mixed in with all the other voices shouting for our attention and energies.

And yet, when we come right down to it, there seems to be an incredible discrepancy between the professed thirst for intimacy and the obviously nonintimate behavior people actually engage in. If this be true, perhaps we have a clue as to why marriages are breaking up and why there is so much anxiety today about the lack of intimacy. One thing we hold as a fairly workable principle in psychotherapy is that when a person's ideal self and his actual self, as he perceives them, are quite a distance apart from each other, he will experience anxiety and other symptoms of personality nonintegration.

The same principle applies to intimacy. If our ideal is to experience a lot of intimacy and if we feel that we do not experience much intimacy, then we will experience marked anxiety and also other symptoms of a conflicted person. That seems to be the situation with intimacy today. The media stimulates us to *want* more intimacy. It helps to create within us an almost insatiable need for intimacy. And yet, to blame the media totally for a felt lack of intimacy on the part of many is far too easy. It leaves out a most important factor.

We do it to ourselves! No one else messes us up. A disturbed man once came to see a psychiatrist and said, "Doc, I'm depressed." The psychiatrist responded with, "Cheer up!" The client was taken back by the terse response and wondered if he were spending his dollar-a-minute wisely. After a brittle moment of silence, the psychiatrist went on to elaborate: "There are only two persons in this room, and I certainly do not have the power to cheer you up. *You* are the only one who can do it." The truth was told, even though the "couch-side manner" might have left something to be desired. Now let's see how we sometimes do ourselves in—how we sometimes unconsciously set up the situation to keep ourselves from experiencing intimacy.

Intimidated by Intimacy

If nearly everyone agrees that intimacy is desirable to have, why doesn't the behavior of people reflect what they *say* they want? Students of human behavior keep their attention focused primarily on behavior. We *listen* to the words, of course, but we believe that a person's actual behavior best represents what he really wants to do—at *that* moment of behavior. Apparently then, if we go by observation of human behavior, most people really don't want to experience intimacy—at least in the light of the price they would have to pay to obtain it.

It's easy to blame circumstances or another person for one's predicaments. It was Fritz Perls who remarked that we reach maturity when we are finally able to forgive our parents. This means that when the individual stops blaming others for his circumstances and accepts personal responsibility for who he is and where he is in life, he has "come of age." Perhaps we ourselves really are responsible much of the time for our not achieving intimacy. Here are some deeper reasons why we might set things up so we could not possibly achieve intimacy. When we do this, we win two ways: we avoid intimacy, and we can also blame others or the circumstances (we have set up) for our not achieving intimacy.

1. Some people relate to other persons in terms of power or control. Therefore, to engage in the intimacy of self-disclosure, for example, arouses too many fears within the individual that he will lose the power he has with another person. He fears letting himself become too vulnerable and giving his competitor (paradoxically his potentially intimate other) a way of hurting him or getting to him. Since he lives by power, he projects that motivation upon others, also. Of course, what he doesn't realize is that power behavior elicits power behavior in response. He could de-escalate, but his fears won't let him do that. So he keeps his distance.

2. Some individuals are extremely independent persons.

They do not want to have to set limits on their behavior which they feel a commitment to intimacy with another person would require. They do not want to adjust their wants and needs to the wants and needs of another person. They see compromise as self-limiting. They see occasionally deferring to the wishes of another person as weak and/or as robbing one's self of integrity and independence.

3. Some individuals have so little capacity for empathy that they are never able to cross the chasm between themselves and another person to feel what the other person feels and to understand him deeply. The behavior of the other person is puzzling to them—so the partner never really feels deeply understood.

4. Some individuals are so sensitive to the possibility of experiencing anxiety that they do everything they can to avoid even the possibility of experiencing it. For example, some persons fear getting close enough to another person to get in touch with that person's flaws and weaknesses. These individuals often feel so impotent and weak in themselves that they feel that the only hope they have for continuing stability in the marriage relationship, and in life for that matter, lies in the strengths of the other person. They are operating from the life position, "I'm not OK; you're OK."

For this kind of person to perceive weaknesses in the individual he had counted on so much to get him through life would be frightening indeed. And so he keeps himself at a distance; he overlooks; he denies. He draws his only felt strength from the assumed adequacy of the other person. To get in touch with the *total* personhood of his spouse—which would include her weaknesses too—would undercut his own feelings of security. It would intensify the anxiety he feels rumbling just beneath the levels of his shaky control. "Let sleeping dogs lie," he believes.

5. Some individuals already have so many personal advantages from living with another person in a manipulative

and exploitive relationship that (at some level of consciousness) they think it would be foolish to give up such a life-style in favor of a game-free, open, and deep relationship. Such individuals desire to keep the winning game intact. Why not? Only because of a need for intimacy—if the individual has such a need. He doesn't!

6. Some individuals are so out of touch with themselves that they can neither understand themselves well nor other persons. They blindly set themselves up again and again to lose—and then they often blame other people or the circumstances for their problems. These unfortunate, self-*un*conscious, incongruent people victimize themselves through their impulsive, self-destructive actions. They are fully capable of destroying the love another person might have for them.

7. Some individuals place such a premium on solitude, aloneness, and personal privacy that they just make themselves unavailable to the other person. They are not lonely and do not seem to need other persons. They may even excel in intimacy with themselves and perhaps even in intimacy with God, but they do not let other persons into their self-sufficient world.

8. Some individuals have dedicated and invested themselves so fully in some life endeavor that they don't want to spend the necessary time and energy required to develop an intimate relationship. Although they might not admit it, by their behavior it is clear that these other pursuits have a higher priority in their lives than intimacy with persons.

9. Some individuals back away from the prospects of intimacy because of a fear that, if they were to be able to achieve intimacy with someone, they might then somehow lose that person—perhaps through death. The consequent pain that they *might* experience would be too great to endure, they think. For such people it is *not* better to have loved and lost than never to have loved at all. For them it is safer not to have loved at all. This feeling often is experienced by the formerly married who have lost loved ones through death or divorce.

They are often still in some recovery phase of the grief process.

10. Some individuals have such negative views of themselves that they believe they could not possibly be sufficiently lovable for another person ever to invest himself in them. Thus, the individual avoids the possibility that he might be led on and hurt by another person. He appears cold and unresponsive to honest overtures and affirmations of his value and worth as a person. He is sure that, if he were ever to reach out for intimacy, he would be rejected, so he stays to himself. Often such an individual is so inexperienced in interpersonal relations that he does not feel he would have the skills to handle an intimate relationship, should it ever develop.

11. Some individuals have such emotionally explosive personalities that others are required to "walk on eggs" in their presence and live in an atmosphere of fear and apprehension. Some marital partners achieve a reciprocal neurotic fit and live a life of staying out of one another's way. Others cannot tolerate such a situation, and so the whole marital relationship is characterized by continual conflict. Never being able to cool down the heat of conflict, they are also never able to arise from the ashes of conflict and go on to intimacy. They live in a continuous state of scar wars!

12. Some individuals can never give up the attempt to make the other person fit neatly into his own idealized concept of what his acceptable marital partner would be like. They can never learn to accept the other person for who he is. They can never appreciate the other person's God-given uniqueness. Instead they continue to play the "fitting game" and constantly remind the other person of where he is falling short of what he should be as a spouse. They remain immersed in the fantasies of their childhood dreams.

13. Some individuals have experienced such deep intimacy with another person at some time that they will not permit themselves to experience intimacy with their present spouse. This can happen, for example, when the individual had a deep

experience of intimacy before marriage, before a spouse left (separated or divorced), or before a spouse died. It can also happen with an extramarital affair. The idealized absent person stands between the two psychologically as an impenetrable wall. In a few cases the symbolic figure who stands between is an over-idealized parent figure. No other person can ever quite measure up to this awesome idol. The figure can also come straight out of fantasy—"a knight in shining armor" or a "beautiful princess."

14. Some individuals feel they are so lacking in the skills of communication, verbal and nonverbal, that they are not able to transmit the feelings they have. They do not realize that they probably do much better than they think they do and that communication can only be improved with practice. However, fearing to be seen by others as inadequate, they remain quiet to avoid exposure—and so they actually become or remain inadequate. They have resigned themselves to the proverb: "It is better to remain silent and appear to be a fool than to open your mouth and remove all doubt."

15. Some individuals dislike conflict so much that they are *unwilling* to confront another person when they are uncomfortable with something in the relationship. Instead they "go along" and make peace—at any price! In so doing, although they avoid conflict, they take themselves out of touch with their true feelings. They blind themselves to the anger they have toward the other person. They harbor resentment and it accumulates over a period of time. The result is a loss of feelings of warmth. Conflict is necessary to sweep the floor clean in order to get ready for intimacy to move in. For those who won't deal with conflict, the hope of intimacy is buried in the dirt of indifference.

I think it is easy to see that if these are the major barriers to intimacy, most of the responsibility for the lack of intimacy lies well within the power of the individual. If we do not experience intimacy, we should ask ourselves why. We must ask ourselves if we really *want* to do whatever needs to be done to experience intimacy. He who victimizes himself in many of the above ways *keeps himself* from experiencing intimacy and surely drives a stake through the heart of intimacy with his own hands.

My conclusion is that almost everyone *wants* intimacy, but few want it enough to do what is necessary to achieve the coveted "holy grail." My purpose here has been to lay bare the truth of the matter and thus to encourage people to take or accept responsibility for their not obtaining intimacy. The choice belongs to the individual.

In no sense am I implying here that anyone *should* do whatever is necessary to achieve intimacy. That decision is up to each person. Every one of us has the right to rank his values according to his own priorities. However, we do have a responsibility to be *aware* of what we are doing and why. It must be a decision we make, freely chosen, with all of the facts at hand. Such an awareness may lead to a clarification of our values and a reordering of our priorities with the result that an individual can truly free himself to achieve intimacy. You have the power. You must choose for yourself.

Pseudo-Intimacy

What about couples who profess that they have intimacy but whose behavior belies their contention? What does their behavior look like? Many participate in false, partial, or incomplete relationships which give only the appearance of intimacy. Couples lapse into pseudo-intimacy when they do not admit that they cannot or will not achieve intimacy and yet verbally continue to affirm the value and importance of it in the relationship. They begin to play games which might sound something like: "Look how close we are"; or "We are still just a couple of lovebirds"; or "Every day with Suzy is sweeter than the day before."

Some other forms of pseudo-intimacy include: sexual relations without personal closeness; substitution of the frequency of contact with one's spouse for depth of contact; what the O'Neills call the "couple front"—that is, always having to relate to others as a couple and never as individuals; jealousy games of a petty nature—in order to keep a little action in the marriage; excessive socializing by the couple; the movement toward chemicals to enliven the life of the couple; and anything else that can deafen the thunderous roar of the emptiness of their marriage.

Pseudo-intimacy is a game played by a couple both of whom, at some level of consciousness, prefer the games to an intimate relationship. It is played by those who feel powerless to do anything about the lack of deeply felt closeness in their lives. It is played by those who believe that the other person is incapable of intimacy. Whatever the reason, apparently the pain of admission to the fact that they do not have an intimate relationship is at least somewhat greater than the energy it takes to keep up appearances. At least that's what their behavior seems to say.

Some couples can live like this throughout the entire course of their marriage—a relationship I call "marital malaise." Other individuals, however, will not tolerate this situation forever. They begin to make demands upon their partner to work on the relationship. Some finally leave the marriage in desperation. Others find new life in their marriage as a result of their work.

There is one particularly critical time in a marriage relationship when things seem to come to a head for many couples. This critical period has been called the middle-age crisis. What is special about this time of life? What factors are working to bring about such an upheaval?

The Middle-Age Marital Crisis

I don't devote much space in this book to the development of intimacy during various stages of the life cycle. But I would like to focus briefly on the middle-age crisis because it represents a time in the marriage relationship when the awareness of a lack of intimacy may be at its highest. This crisis refers to a time of life, averaging around age forty, when men and women may experience a kind of alienation from each other. The result is often a feeling of the loss of intimacy. This in turn produces a crisis in the marriage which sometimes ends in divorce. After twenty-five years of married life, everyone is surprised to see the couple separate.

In order to understand this crisis clearly, we must make a distinction between *precipitating* events and *predisposing* factors. Although we observe a number of obvious things which are occurring at or about the same time the crisis hits, we must be careful not to assume that these events and circumstances are the only causes and thus fail to be alert to the possible deeper causes of the crisis.

Some of the surface occurrences we observe are: (a) some or all of the children have gone from the home (the "empty nest"), (b) the menopause in women, and (c) the aging process. There are other possible events which can occur, too, such as an illness, an accident, or a career crisis. Of course, they can occur at any age, but these fortuitous events may trigger deeper processes at this particular age. These surface occurrences are more of the nature of *precipitating* events than basic causes, in most cases. But there might be a more fundamental *predisposing* factor which gives power to the events above to trigger in a person such a reaction as the middle-age marital crisis. What might that predisposing factor be?

I see the middle-age crisis fundamentally as an *existential* crisis—an intense refocusing on the nature and meaning of one's own existence. I have seen people experience this crisis as early as the thirties and as late as the fifties. I do not believe it is a biological event. Although the menopause in women and the natural aging process are associated with the event, they may serve only as catalysts to the more basic reaction.

The critical predisposing factor, in my opinion, is the growing awareness that the *nature* of one's existence is changing and that the meaning of one's self-definition is threatened. Aging then would be an important factor triggering this awareness. But it is not chronological age which triggers the reaction; rather it is *perceived* aging that does it. It is how one *thinks* that the aging process threatens the *nature* of his existence. That is why the crisis occurs earlier for some and later for others.

It is not life itself that is threatened, rather the way one looks at himself—how he sees himself as a person. A person is threatened existentially when what he thinks produces his happiness is in danger of being lost. And so if a person sees himself as youthful, vigorous, and attractive, aging will challenge this self-definition and threaten the individual existentially.

It can happen like this too: an individual, from his own private perceptual vantage point, arrives psychologically in his process of development at the point where he is able to cast his eyes "over the hill" and "down" to what he guesses will be the final years of his life. He makes a prophetic projection in his mind to the place he thinks he may end up in his life. Although some are not disappointed in the vision they see, others are deeply distressed. Some are so shaken that they experience various levels of depression. They feel a sense of desperation and sometimes even panic at their slipping self-perception.

But even if a person is not disappointed with his projection, he still may become sensitive to the fact that he is growing old. He may begin to focus upon the awarenesses that time is getting short, that his physical abilities are declining, that he is becoming less attractive. He may become extremely restless and agitated within. Then, since one goes around only once in this life, he may decide that he is going to make sure that he will make the most of it! Some individuals re-evaluate their whole life situation, including their marriage, to be sure that what they have now is something they will want for themselves the rest of their lives. Some people arrive at a negative conclusion regarding their marriage and decide to divorce and/or to take up an alternate life–style.

Behind it all may be the felt threat to the kind of existence the individual *thinks* he wants for himself. He has a sense of urgency to try to pack into his life all the experiences he can so that later in his life he will not feel cheated. This is what often happens during a typical middle-age crisis. Prevention takes the form of efforts at marriage enrichment and personal awareness of what happens to people during this time of life. Sometimes a counselor is needed to help a person maintain perspective and to help him process what is happening to him.

Sometimes this crisis is triggered by what has come to be called the "empty-nest syndrome." This descriptive phrase refers to the time in a couple's lives when the last of the children have gone from the home, and they begin to experience a feeling of emptiness. One cause of this problem is that they have invested so much time and energy in their children and so little in their marriage that a vacuum has been created. They have pretty much *defined* themselves as parents, not as persons who *do parenting* as one of their several functions. Thus, when the children begin to leave home, the couple is emptied of a major part of their self–definition. They are forced to experience each other again for the first time in a long time as marital partners—not as "Mom" and "Dad." They may feel uncomfortable in this continuing relationship because they have failed to work on intimacy in their marriage. There seems to be nothing surviving between them as a couple quite big enough to fill up the space the departing of their children has created. They are faced with the stark reality that they have become strangers to each other. Many times the shock is too great for the marriage relationship to survive.

In order to prevent the empty-nest syndrome from occurring,

one needs to work not only on marriage enrichment but also on personal enrichment. Individuals who have defined themselves almost exclusively in terms of being a parent are bound to suffer an identity crisis when the reasons for their existence—their children—leave the home. We must be careful to define ourselves as complex human beings, capable of *many* important functions. We must accordingly cultivate many interests. We probably should invest ourselves in some life mission important to us. Then when the children leave home, only part of our mission as persons is concluded. We can reinvest the energy we previously had been giving to the children into the other pursuits we have been developing all along. This can enrich a person's life considerably and make him a more interesting marital partner at the same time.

Intimacy As a Growth Need

Most people have been introduced to the need theory of Maslow[2] which separates human needs into two broad categories: those which provide a kind of *maintenance* function and those which provide *growth* for the individual. Briefly, a maintenance need is one which will not make the individual happy, but if it is not present, it certainly will make him unhappy. The maintenance needs include: physiological needs, safety needs, belongingness needs, and esteem needs. This is also how Maslow ranks the needs, from lowest to highest, in terms of the demands made upon us for attention and energy. The theory proposes that when the lowest needs are satisfied, we are set free to pursue the next highest need.

The growth needs are those which make a person happy when they are obtained but do not necessarily make the individual unhappy if they are not obtained. Maslow suggested that among the growth needs are: the need for intellectual pursuits and the need for aesthetic experience. If one does not participate much in these higher growth functions, life certainly will continue, but it will take on a rather bland and blah flavor.

Those who are meeting the growth needs in their lives are self-actualizing. My definition of self-actualization is "to make continual, significant progress toward becoming all one may be." Those who meet only their maintenance needs are just functioning. They are neither happy nor unhappy.

Maslow's theory is a model—a conceptual analogue of the truth of reality. Models make it easier to think about and talk about something very complex. They are convenient fictions which help us dialogue about a difficult subject. As such we do not respond appropriately to a model when we attack or criticize it. The question is not whether it is true or false. The only valid question to ask about a model is whether it helps us more easily discuss something extremely complex. While Maslow's model was not meant to be applied to intimacy, I believe the model can be useful in helping us understand intimacy at this point.

If we were to extend Maslow's model so it would include the transactional or interpersonal element, we could add intimacy to the list of Maslow's growth needs. Intimacy definitely is a growth need in a relationship. All other interactions in a relationship are mere maintenance functions. This explains why we can spend a lot of time with someone and yet not achieve intimacy. We can relate to the other in many different areas of life and yet not achieve intimacy. We can talk about many ideas and concepts and make a lot of plans together and yet not achieve intimacy. *Intimacy is something extra!* It goes to the core of being. It does not content itself to wander endless miles in the wasteland of meaningless chatter.

To reach for intimacy is to struggle with it desperately through the long night hours as Jacob wrestled with the angel (Gen. 32:24–28). And just as Jacob did not let the angel go until the angel had blessed him, so those who would seek intimacy cannot make a halfhearted attempt. One must invest all! And—to press the biblical analogy one last step—just as Jacob paid the price of a permanent weakness in his hip for his efforts, so the seeker after intimacy will pay a price for his efforts. He will have to give up other things such as shallowness, selfishness, and an inordinate achievement orientation. The price is different for everyone, but intimacy yields its sweet fruit only to the committed.

How Many Couples Have an Intimate Relationship?

The kinds of questions couples ask about intimacy include the following: "Are we failing to achieve the amount of intimacy we *should* in our marriage?" "Are we missing out on what most other couples are *regularly* experiencing?" "Is there something more we could do to achieve intimacy in our marriage?" "Are we a *normal* couple with respect to the ability to achieve intimacy?" "How much intimacy *should* be enough for a couple? Perhaps we are wanting too much." I strongly believe that each couple should decide for themselves how much is enough, and they should set up their own "shoulds."

Individuals differ in their need for intimacy because of how they were raised and because of their own unique temperaments. Some people are what might be called "high need-for-contact persons" while others are what might be called "low need-for-contact persons." (Of course, there is also the large majority of persons in the middle who need to avoid either extreme.) The descriptive phrase, high need-for-contact, might be interpreted as meaning either a need for *many* contacts or as a need for *deep* and meaningful contacts. I am referring here to the depth (the qualitative) dimension rather than to the number of contacts when I speak of high and low need-for-contact persons.

So then, high need-for-*depth*-contact persons have a tendency to seek out intimate relationships actively. But just to *be* a high need-for-depth-contact person by temperament and/or training is not sufficient. One must also have enough social self-confidence and psychological toughness to risk the inevitable interpersonal failures or rejections which are likely to occur as one seeks for this kind of relationship. Finally, the high need-for-depth-contact person must also have a sufficient amount of energy to invest in building the kind of depth relationship he would like to have.

There are some people who clearly are afraid of intimacy; they almost seem to work actively to avoid it. It is not by chance or because of bad luck that they do not experience intimacy. At some level of consciousness, the deepest self of such persons knows that, should they begin to get close to another person, they would not be able to handle it. And so typically this person enters a cycle: first, driven by deep and natural needs for human attachment, he moves toward another; but the closer he gets the more anxious he becomes until he finally turns and runs away. But then, moving into another in-and-out cycle, he feels the need to move closer again to someone and the cycle is repeated.

These are the people who go from relationship to relationship, sometimes through one engagement after another, and sometimes from one marriage into another marriage. The whole thing amounts to a conflict between the need for human attachment and the fear of intimacy. John Powell caught the essence of this fear of intimacy in his book *Why Am I Afraid to Tell You Who I Am?*[3]

Perhaps it is clearer now why intimacy may not be a frequent occurrence even in good marriages, especially if one or both are high achievers, are low in energy, and/or are threat sensitive. Some individuals wait, as did Cinderella, for some fairy godmother to come along and lay all their hoped-for dreams in their laps without their having to turn a hand. Unlike Cinderella, however, they may just continue to sit among the cinders and ashes until they decide to get up, bless themselves, and begin to work to develop the kind of relationship they would like to have.

Assuming that the definition of intimacy I gave at the beginning of this work is an acceptable one, how many couples experience intimacy in their marriage on a fairly regular basis? Let us assume that the kind of intimacy we are talking about is not just superficial levels of closeness. The conclusion we would reach might be very different depending upon the assumptions we make. If we insist that intimacy is a special human event and include the restrictions I mentioned above, we will arrive at a lower figure than we would if we were not to make such assumptions.

A Hypothesis About How Often Intimacy Is Achieved

I would like to offer a *hypothesis* about the frequency of intimacy in marriages. It is only a hypothesis, for there is really no hard evidence to support it. But perhaps there are some suggestions for it in the writings of those who have studied intimacy.

I will include as a part of my hypothesis the description of five different types of marriage relationships offered by Cuber and Harroff.[4] Their model is derived from a study of affluent couples married for ten years or more. They identified the following marital relationship patterns:

(a) *The conflict-habituated marriage* in which hostility was expressed chronically through fighting.
(b) *The devitalized marriage* in which intimacy once did exist but now it has ceased to exist and the zest is gone.
(c) *The passive-congenial marriage* in which intimacy never did exist, and the relationship is characterized as being quiet, polite, and convenient.
(d) *The vital marriage* in which intimacy is still experienced more than occasionally.
(e) *The total marriage* in which the couple has so many areas of commonality and the relationship is so deep and vivid that intimacy is experienced quite often.

Now, assuming that intimacy is a special or rare experience, that intimacy is a growth need, and that the Cuber and Harroff patterns are at least a useful description of the various kinds of marriages, I would propose the hypothesis represented by the diagram below.

ALL MARRIAGE RELATIONSHIPS					
.1 2	16	50 84	98	99.9	Percentiles
Conflict-Habituated 10%	Devitalized 20%	Passive-Congenial 60%	Vital 8%	Total 2%	Cuber and Harroff 60%
Maintenance (Surface Relating and Pseudo-intimacy)			Growth (Intimacy)		Maslow

Supposed Occurrence of Intimacy in Marriages

Implications of the Hypothesis

What are the implications for intimacy in the hypothesis? First let's look more intently at the Cuber and Harroff patterns. What I have to say here is my own view of how such a marital pattern might function. I am not reporting Cuber and Harroff's findings, but only using their descriptive labeling. I see the conflict-habituated couples as feeling trapped in the marriage. Of course, they are getting *something* out of it or they would not stay in the marriage. What these binding factors are might be very intriguing. It is probably safe to say that there is a neurotic element in one or both of the individuals for them to be willing to endure such continual stress. They may be rigidly bound into the marriage by the expectations of others and are slowly killing each other psychologically by their constant release of frustration and anger onto each other.

The devitalized marriage is probably a painful marriage since they once saw what could be and now they are painfully aware that intimacy no longer exists. This marriage pattern may be moving toward a divorce or into either the conflict-habituated or the next pattern we shall discuss—the passive-congenial pattern.

The passive-congenial pattern probably describes most marriages, in my opinion. Both individuals are fairly comfortable living with each other. They often have invested themselves in the material things of life to such an extent that the material loss if they were to separate would be severe. This material investment may not be the only bond, but it is a strong deterrent to divorce. The couple may have strong beliefs about the family, and the presence of children produces another bond which they may find difficult to consider breaking. They may have other life pursuits into which they have poured themselves in order to drown out the cries of their need for intimacy. They may have strong religious convictions about divorce.

It is also typical of such a relationship that they have learned not to confront the other person when they are upset or uncomfortable about some aspect of the relationship. Because of this, all hope of conflict resolution has been buried. Instead, the two learn to "roll with the punches" and try not to irritate or annoy the other. Such individuals often describe their spouses as more like a friend or a family member than as an intimate partner. Sometimes they describe the other as being like a sister or a brother. Such couples may have high enough defenses so that they do not feel the emptiness of their relationship.

I have grouped the vital and total patterns together because they involve at least some amount of intimacy. Probably the degree and amount of intimacy experienced in these two patterns is a function more of the amount of energy available and the degree of need-for-depth contact in the individuals rather than of a differential capacity to achieve intimacy. If both individuals have high needs for intimacy, the pattern is more likely to be the total pattern. Intimacy, in this case, would be so important to both of them that they would be willing to put aside most other claims for their attention and energy and to put the experience of intimacy first among their priorities. I also believe this pattern is rare.

Another implication which follows from the hypothesis is that I attribute the relational *growth* of intimacy only to the vital and the total marital patterns. The other three patterns can only be *maintenance* levels of relational functioning. Marital happiness *with respect to intimacy* is only achieved in these two fairly rare marital patterns.

One point needs further clarification. I am not saying that marital *happiness* is rare, only that marital happiness *with respect to the amount of intimacy achieved in the marriage* is not frequent. People marry and stay married for many reasons. The meeting of intimacy needs is only *one* of those reasons. If what I am saying about intimacy is true, it is not a commonly *achieved* goal of marriage, although it may well be a typical aspiration of those who marry.

I believe there are many couples who, as individuals, can say that they are truly happy in their marriage. It does *not* follow in my mind that they are achieving intimacy. It could mean that the marriage is congenial and friendly, that the two are working together for some common goals, that they meet each other's sexual and relational needs, and that in this relationship each finds that he can meet her personal growth needs. But there may be little or no intimacy. So it should be clearly understood that I am not referring to marital happiness, in general, in this discussion, rather to marital happiness only as it relates to the meeting of intimacy needs.

My hypothesis is that not many people experience intimacy, although most people profess that they would like to. Not every person is even capable of achieving intimacy as discussed in chapter 3. Apparently, from observing the behavior of people, most couples are not willing to set aside the necessary time and to invest sufficient energy to improve their capacity for intimacy or to work on intimacy with their partner. As a result, few couples achieve much intimacy often. That has to be my conclusion. I find no writers who disagree with what

I am saying here, although they do not state the case as pointedly as I do.

Given the basic capacity for intimacy, the achievement of intimacy becomes a matter of decision and commitment. Intimacy remains for most couples an ideal to strive for. Intimacy is what most couples say they would like to have but for which little effective effort is in fact expended. Of course, many will offer "reasons" (excuses or rationalizations) which they say keep them from experiencing intimacy—as though it were not their fault. But intimacy is there for the taking *if* one chooses to reach out for it. It is within our power in most cases.

A Difficult Dilemma: The Crucible

What if one person does want intimacy in the relationship but the other one does not? Or, what if one person is fully capable of achieving at least some amount of intimacy but the other person is not? What then? What if one person, to whom intimacy has been a stranger for a long time and from whom the memory of its bliss has almost faded, seemingly out of nowhere, has a soul-touching experience with another person? This event then revives the memory and the desire to renew the pursuit of intimacy. But what if the partner doesn't want to work on intimacy? These are difficult matters.

The dilemma is to stay in a nonintimate but otherwise comfortable marriage or to divorce and *hope* to achieve intimacy with someone else. A difficult dilemma! It is a crucible! We watch such persons suffering in the afternoon soap dramas; we also meet these individuals in the counseling office. They look for a way out of their dilemma, but they see only "No Exit" signs! They will not stand for moralistic advice. The simple answers are sufficient only for those who are not experiencing the problem. To those in the valley of conflict the easy solutions sound hollow and irrelevant—like sounding brass and tinkling cymbal.

I certainly have no easy answer. However, I do suggest that the one experiencing the pain of the lack of intimacy confront his partner with his feelings. There will be discomfort, of course, and there may be no solution to the problem which is acceptable to both. But at least the real issue will be out in the open. Only then can it be dealt with in whatever way is acceptable to the couple. It is their issue and their decision. They must do the choosing.

The Continuing Quest

Despite the fact that few actually achieve intimacy, people still press on toward the goal of an intimate relationship. *I believe the quest is worth it!* The picture I have painted is not very optimistic, and the journey I have mapped out toward intimacy is an arduous one, but we must first know the task that lies before us if we are to make realistic plans for our journey.

If a person decides that intimacy is really worth the effort and decides to commence the journey, he should first make a joint commitment with his spouse to *work* on it continually. Nothing less will do the job! Even if a couple is discouraged, amazing things can happen. Feeling might now be buried beneath boredom, resentment, and much frustration, but it still might be possible to dig it up and bring feeling back to life.

Many married couples who thought feelings were dead have surprised themselves. They have witnessed a beautiful phoenix arising in their lives, dug up from the smoldering ashes of what both feared was the final funeral pyre of intimacy in their marriage. Such resurrections are encouraging. There is no way to know how often this happens in marriages, but it's healing and hope-inspiring to know that such things do occasionally occur.

On the other hand, there is also a grim side to the story. It is possible to let feeling lie buried too long—until all life-support systems for intimacy have failed and nothing remains except interment. Such an awareness underscores the importance of early intervention through counseling and marriage enrichment endeavors.

Although intimacy is a voluntary, mutual, interpersonal relationship, it does have to start somewhere. Someone has to initiate it. Only occasionally is there a mutual coming together; more often one person reaches out first. It requires some assertiveness on your part if you are to raise the probabilities of experiencing intimacy in your own life. If you argue you *can't,* ask yourself if it isn't actually true that you *won't.* Take responsibility for that. *You* will have to strive for intimacy most of the time. What do you *want* to do? Are you willing to reach out for intimacy?

What Do You Think?

1. Discuss your reaction to the case of Bill and Mary. Did you like them as persons? What did you dislike about them? Where did they make mistakes regarding intimacy—as best you can guess with so little specific information? What do you think they decided to do about intimacy at the end of the discussion of the case?

2. Identify and discuss with your intimate other the three greatest strengths in your marriage and also the three most obvious weaknesses or areas which need the most work.

3. Discuss privately with your intimate other where you two fall on the chart which shows my hypothesis about how many couples actually are experiencing an intimate marriage. What do you need to do in order to achieve a more intimate relationship if you fall at a place on the continuum where you feel you need to make a change?

4. What is your reaction to my hypothesis about the number of people experiencing intimacy in marriage? Do you think that many more experience intimacy than I have suggested—

assuming an acceptance of the definition I use, and assuming we are not talking about "marital happiness"?

5. Make plans for an "Intimacy Honeymoon"—a week or two away together—just the two of you with no other agenda than to draw closer to each other and to work on the development of intimacy in your relationship.

6. Make some very specific plans for the near future to take some weekends away in order to work on the marriage. Take no one with you and let the relationship be the only agenda. Set a calendar date right now. Decide together how often this needs to be done—every month, every six weeks, or every two months.

Notes

Chapter One

1. Clarence L. Barnhart, ed., *The American College Dictionary* (New York: Random House, 1953).

2. Philip Babcock Gove, ed., *Webster's Third New International Dictionary of the English Language, Unabridged* (Springfield, Mass.: G. & C. Merriam Co., Publishers, 1976).

3. *Webster's Seventh New Collegiate Dictionary* (Springfield, Mass.: G. & C. Merriam Co., Publishers, 1976).

4. Thomas C. Oden, *Game Free: A Guide to the Meaning of Intimacy* (New York: Harper and Row, 1974), p. 12.

5. Mignon McLaughlin, *The Neurotic's Notebook* (New York: Bobbs Merrill Co., Inc., 1963), p. 11.

6. Ibid., p. 19.

Chapter Two

1. McLaughlin, *The Neurotic's Notebook,* p.13.

Chapter Three

1. Howard J. Clinebell, Jr. and Charlotte H. Clinebell, *The Intimate Marriage* (New York: Harper and Row, 1970), pp. 28–32.

2. Gordon W. Allport, *Pattern and Growth in Personality* (New York: Holt, Rinehart and Winston, Inc., 1961), pp. 384–387.

3. Ibid., pp. 533–537.

4. Carl R. Rogers, *On Becoming a Person* (Boston: Houghton-Mifflin Co., 1961), pp. 50–55.

5. Ibid., p. 52.

6. Allport, *Pattern and Growth,* p. 261.

Chapter Four

1. Clinebell and Clinebell, *The Intimate Marriage,* pp. 28–32.

2. Sherrod Miller et al., *Alive and Aware* (Minneapolis: Interpersonal Communication Programs, Inc., 1975).

3. John Bear, *The World's Worst Proverbs* (Los Angeles: Price/Stern/Sloan, Publishers, Inc., 1976), p. 14.

4. Gordon Allport, *The Individual and His Religion* (New York: The Macmillan Co., 1950), p. 142.

Chapter Five

1. Nena and George O'Neill, *Open Marriage* (New York: M. Evans, 1972), p. 162.

2. Abraham H. Maslow, *Motivation and Personality* (New York: Harper and Row, 1970), pp. 35–58.

3. John Powell, *Why Am I Afraid to Tell You Who I Am?* (Niles, Ill.: Argus Communications, 1969).

4. John Cuber and Peggy Harroff, *The Significant Americans* (New York: Appleton-Century, 1965).